Football Voodoo

Magic, superstition and re

F&M Publications

To Joanne

Published by F&M Publications May 2010

www.fandmpublications.co.uk
F&M Publications
PO BOX 51243
London SE17 3WP
www.footyvoodoo.com

Illustrations by Daniel Morgenstern   www.danielmorgenstern.com
Cover photographs by Andrew Buurman   www.buurman.co.uk/

Design: Gary Lingard

A CIP catalogue record for this book is available from the British Library.

ISBN-13: 978-0-9564940-1-6
ISBN-(ebook): 978-0-9564940-2-3

Contents

Foreword

I't'll probably come as no surprise that the idea for *Football Voodoo* occurred to me in a pub. More specifically, and less obviously, in a room above a pub in Holborn whilst a witch explained how she prepared for a ritual. As I listened to her describe how she focused her mind, donned a sacred kit and kissed a symbol before entering a special marked off space for some reason the image of Wayne Rooney kissing the Newton Heath crest at Goodison popped into my mind. So began a chain of thought that led to the book. How I managed to mentally jump from a flame headed wiccan in Central London to a talented lad from Liverpool 11 with a low centre of gravity is something that I'll probably let psychologists work out if I ever make enough money to afford proper psychiatric care.

Psychology weaves its way through the book and many practices that could be regarded as superstitious, religious or even obsessive compulsive have a sound psychological and in the case of colour, evolutionary biological, underpinning. In this way the research meandered away from straight forward witchcraft and folkways into sports psychology and various associations of symbols, colours and numbers which naturally are something football has in superabundance. There is also the question of chanting and the impact of prayer so it seemed foolish not to add in something on, what must today be referred to as, the terrace anthem or indeed the priestly aphorisms of the manager. The aim has been to provide an overview of all of these areas, hopefully without repetition and too much reliance on the foibles of contemporary superstars.

There is no attempt to cover all superstitions in the game and naturally with a subject like this fresh stories are being reported all the time which we are trying to catch on the website (www.footyvoodoo.com). It also means that over the past few years there have been many rewrites, additions and subtractions as well as tactical re-arrangements. However I hope this is the best formation and that what you have is entertaining but solid at the back as well as providing a lot of good stories to kick about.

Chris Roberts
May 2010

Introduction

Before kick off

It's odd to think that the multi million pound business that is modern football started out as an English folk custom on Saints' Days that still take place on Shrove Tuesday in some locations. The thousand a sides which kings complained interfered with archery practice has evolved to become a (relatively) disciplined global sport of eleven versus eleven. The same level of popularity or inroads into the consciousness of the world have not been achieved by, let's say, Morris Dancing or Jack on the Green rituals with which football shares its raucous roots linked to the pagan traditions of the British Isles.

Authorities about mysterious and paranormal Britain, Janet and Colin Bord, even attempt to link football very directly to fertility rituals. Particularly when those magical rites are performed at prehistoric sites, though let's immediately dismiss the coincidence of shape between Stonehenge and goalposts. However Shrove Tuesday was a spring festival well before Christianity and, as the last day of carnival, fitted rather well with a bit of footy related chaos. According to Mircea Eliade, in *Patterns of Comparative Religion.*

> 'The contest and fights which take place in so many places in the
> spring or at harvest time undoubtedly derive from the primitive
> notion that blows, contests, rough games between the sexes and so on,
> all stir up and increase the energies of the whole universe.'

Mob (or should that be total?) football between neighbouring settlements involving an unlimited number of players was a feature of saints' days. The idea of these matches was to shift an inflated pig's bladder, or other object, where one's opponents didn't want it to go. Everyone was at it, so much so that by 1314 the Lord Mayor of London issued a decree banning football on the grounds of civic disorder and that it might offend God. Fifty years later King Edward III followed up with a prohibition on 'idle games' including football and a half century later Henry IV forbad the charging of money for football.

A later King, Henry VIII, ordered boots but no one is sure exactly what position he played and there is further royal approval from James I's Book of Sports (1618) that instructs Christians to play at football every Sunday afternoon after worship. Other reports are less positive as the game is associated, in a shockingly accurate foretelling of events 400 years later, with disorder by authorities in Manchester. In 1608 they complained that: 'With the football...[there] hath beene great disorder in our towne of Manchester we are told, and glasse windowes broken yearlye and spoyled by a companie of lewd and disordered persons'. Shakespeare was also clearly not a fan referring to a character in King Lear as a 'base football player'

The game though moved from being part of the mob's ritual through the class structure and it was really the English public schools that were responsible for codifying the rules of modern football and for organizing it into a competitive team sport. The shift to a more disciplined working culture, at least in terms of regular hours, as well as the length of time worked and a decline in traditional holidays meant that feast day street football decreased. The public schools though kept developing the game, or games as they began to split up different sets of rules into Rugby and Association Football amongst others. Better communications meant moves towards standardization were possible including in 1848 at Cambridge the introduction of the offside rule. Players in Sheffield developed a separate code in the late 1850s, which was responsible for many innovations. These included free kicks, corner kicks, handball, throw-ins and the crossbar.

When the Football Association formed at the Freemason's Tavern, Great Queen Street, London in 1863 they created the London rules based on the old Cambridge ones, which tellingly still contained some acceptance of handling the ball. Later, in 1877, much of the Sheffield code was incorporated and the adoption of the combined set by Sheffield and Nottingham (now Notts County) and later Chesterfield and Stoke spread the codified form across the country and to all classes (a job done even more efficiently in Scotland by Queens Park). William

McGregor, a director of Aston Villa, was the main force behind the formation of a league competition in 1888 that merged with the rival Football Alliance in 1892 enabling two divisions to form. The early clubs were often church or work teams as the game gradually moved away from its public school associations back into the mass event that it started out as.

Put more succinctly; a rowdy ritual on saints' days becomes upper class with rules codified at a pub frequented by members of a secret society. The church becomes involved as does big business and the game is sold back to the masses in a much neater form. Anthropologist Desmond Morris thinks that football evolved from the pack hunt and taps into the very origins of human life. In the Soccer Tribes he writes: 'Viewed in this way, a game of football becomes a reciprocal hunt. Each team of players, or 'hunting pack', tries to score a goal by aiming a ball, or 'weapon' at a defended goal-mouth, or 'prey'. The essence of the ancient hunting pattern was that it involved a great deal of physical exercise combined with risk and excitement. It involved a long sequence with a build-up, with strategy and planning, with skill and daring and ultimately with a grand climax and a moment of triumph.'

Amusing though the notion of say Robin Van Persie heading up a group to hunt wild boar might be the links that Desmond Morris makes between team sports and a ritualised form of hunting are apt. The modern sport is much more scientifically focused relying on diet, fitness, isotonic drinks and precisely honed tactics but still there are areas of the game that remain irresolutely irrational and certainly laden with symbolism. There are spiritual and psychological issues for players relating to confidence, appetite and concentration, or the various mind games employed by managers. The importance of what's in the mind in terms of belief and confidence as well as the ability to head the ball or intelligently read a match is part of the essence of football. Former Scottish International, Pat Nevin, even wrote a book about it entitled *In Ma Head, Son.* Further evidence is offered by Sven Goren Eriksson who relates stories of footballers having a virtually hundred per cent record when it came to taking penalties in training which fell away to sixty percent in matches. He also noticed discrepancies between what he described as big matches as opposed to 'ordinary' ones with hit ratios declining in the more important games.

With such importance attached to the mental side of the game football is naturally full of tricks and strategies to boost one's own team or weaken opponents. Also rife are various forms of what Sir James Frazer (author of the seminal study of magic and religion, The Golden Bough) would describe as magical thinking. Frazer would also recognize the tribal and primitive religious roots of many of the activities that players practice before a match. Sir James suggested that magical thinking is dependent on two laws to do with similarity; that an effect resembles its cause and also the notion of contagion. The latter is a belief that things that were once in physical contact maintain a connection even after that link has been broken. This is the basis of sympathetic magic and goes some way towards clarifying why West Bromwich fans pat Jeff Astle's image at the gates dedicated to him on their way into the Hawthorns. It also explains the hope that the manipulation of effigies, symbols or tokens can cause changes to occur in the thing the symbol represented. At one extreme there are the use of voodoo fetishes and at Manchester City end a stuffed toy horse.

Some might argue that football is a matter of money, management and fitness and this all a bunch of mumbo jumbo but how many football fans have never said a prayer, performed a ritual or issued a curse? The answer, of course, is none. Then there are the players, managers and other officials to consider with their quirks, odd beliefs and insane utterances which go way beyond magic realism and off into the realms of the fantastic. Former Welsh international Dai Davies has become a medium and believes in reincarnation. He is also quoted as saying, 'there are fairies somewhere with tremendous energy. I can sense angels.' Not everyone goes as far down the alternative religious route as Dai but this book is about the space where faith meets feet and also individuals and their foibles, confidence and temperament.

Former manager Lawrie McMenamy described the perfect football team psychologically as seven road sweepers and four concert violinists. This is pretty astute when one considers how much comment in football is devoted to confidence and how often winning is really a question of faith or commitment, along with touches of magic. Mood determination, confidence, desire and will are all factors that allow toggerists to 'play above themselves.' Many of the sport's best clichés relate to mental, rather than physical, fitness. Graham Taylor and Kevin Keegan, two former

England managers and masters of the nonsensical emotional outburst gifted the world; 'Gary always weighed up his options, especially when he had no choice' and from Graham: 'to be really happy, we must throw our hearts over the bar and hope that our bodies will follow.'

Inspirational pronouncements, such as these, have as much to do with the realms of psychology and appearance over reality, magic in other words, than the physical effort to win a game. If mood and confidence did not have an influence why are there so many tricks used by players and managers alike to unsettle opponents? These range from the relatively obvious diving, shirt pulling and off the ball incidents to giving phoney information about tactics and the injury status of key stars up to such whodunit classics as Bobby Moore and the emerald necklace. In what should have been an episode of Scooby Doo, but was really an attempt to destabilise the England team, Bobby Moore was accused of stealing an emerald necklace in Colombia during training for the 1970 World Cup. Then there was the experience of Fred Ford, erstwhile Bristol City manager, who lost a few of his team before an important match after the squad were all put up in a hotel next to a heavily advertised brothel.

Given the lengths that those involved in football are prepared to go in order to gain a slippery advantage it should come as no surprise that they might also resort to magic of various shades. Many players have unvarying rituals they perform before matches whether to do with dressing, eating, visiting the toilet, entering the pitch or leaving the changing room. Others have lucky boots, shin pads, coins, clothes or aftershave. In what amounts to an almost fetishlike, or possibly obsessive – compulsive condition, top players will arrange objects to face front and tie their laces in a prescribed fashion. They do this in the name of mental preparation, in the superstitious belief that their ritual will enhance how they perform on the pitch. The largest proportion of these involves the dressing room but nearly a fifth take place on the way to the ground and a quarter either in the tunnel or on the pitch itself.

For traditionalists like Italy's Giovanni Trapattoni it is a question of sprinkling holy water on the field. Not everyone has a nun for a sister to provide that so France coach, Raymond Domenech checked out star signs to guide him in his team selection. In an attempt to make every game a home tie in the 2002 World Cup the Costa Rica team spread soil from the country's seven provinces on the pitch. These are classic superstitions with both the notion of holy water cleansing and blessing an area and native soil giving strength abroad popularised through books and films on the vampire legend amongst others. All of which make Germany's 2004 refusal to stay on the 13th floor of a Lisbon hotel quite understandable really.

Football has frequently been referred to as a religion with many clubs being founded by religious orders and others keeping a specific faith as a key part of their identity. A number of fans elect to have a favourite football ground as their final resting place. The chant I'm Carlisle till I die takes on extra meaning when one considers the possibility of the scattering of ashes on the pitch at Brunton Park. Making it possible to be Carlisle after death too, but only if you've been really sinful. Then there is that old Bill Shankly hee haw about football being more serious than life or death anyway. There are miracles, such as how Pele stopped a war in Nigeria as hostilities between Biafra and Nigeria were halted for two days so both sides could watch him play. Then there is the gathering of the relics of a smashed crossbar as if they were pieces of the true cross as happened in Wageningen in Holland and with Scottish fans at Wembley. Some might argue that football has replaced the church as the last place of communal hymn singing but it might be more accurate to suggest that the pop songs adopted before games instead of hymns (as was traditional) is not secularising the game but rather it's apparent that the reverse is true. Certain hits are becoming hymns such as Birmingham City's Keep Right On to the End of the Road for example or Stoke City with Delilah. Port Vale have The Wonder of You, Manchester City Blue Moon and Bristol Rovers Goodnight Irene.

The songs give the fans an additional identity, which is appropriate because football is something tribal, passionate and hard wired into the evolution of mankind making it hardly surprising that some other traits from the past have crept in as well. These might be ancient superstitions, folk religions or magical thinking and ritual behaviour that can give the edge in any high-pressurized competitive situation. Numerous teams have used hypnotism, perhaps most notably, and with the greatest success, Tottenham Hotspur against Leeds in 1975 in a match that saved them from relegation. Then there is the use of colour, symbols and invocation of elders right the way up to hiring mediums, witches and shamans or attempting jinxes in a bid to change the course of a side's fortunes. This is a world of hexed grounds, unlucky shirts, magic horses and burying cattle under goalposts. A place where managers urinate on corner flags and dog mascots on defenders, where players touch images of mythical beasts and exorcists are invited to cleanse pitches. This is Football Voodoo.

Those were the days my friend
Sacred turf and cursed grounds

For those unfamiliar with classic hooligan remakes of Mary Hopkin's songs, the lyrics go:

> Those were the days my friend, we took the Stretford End,
> We ran the Shed, the North Bank Highbury too.
> We'd go wherever we'd choose, we'd fight and never lose,
> Those were the days, oh yes those were the days.

Time marches on and Highbury's North Bank is now flats for the extremely well off whereas the Shed requires a mortgage sized payment to enter and is half given up to away fans anyway. Every team has their home end within the ground where the loudest of their supporters gather. This is a fiefdom, or holy of holies, from the Bebington Kop Tranmere to the Manchester Road Bury (where away supporters have the Cemetery End). During what has been referred to as the golden age of football hooliganism, the late 1960s to mid 1980s, it was the avowed intention of sections of the away support to 'take' the home end or cause the home fans to 'run'.

Taking of a rival team's home end and either marking it in some way or physically removing parts of it – including bits of home supporter's clothing such as scarves – are simply the football fan's continuation of the plundering tradition of all invaders. Rules as to what constituted 'taking' did fluctuate, though. For some, it was enough to establish a presence by chanting or showing colours (the equivalent of planting a flag) before moving on. To the more vigorous, it meant a proper 'off', with large-scale damage or the police resorting to dividing the home end for the whole match. Occasionally the marking could be achieved imaginatively, as Preston North End did at Wrexham in the late 1970s simply by taking over the food shed and bombarding the

Welshmen with ketchup and hot dogs for an extended period prior to kick off.

Some traditionalists would argue that much of the ritual aspect of football violence has been removed now that fights tend to occur at out of town shopping centres or other unholy venues. However, in *Avenues of Contestation: Football Hooligans Running and Ruling Urban Spaces,* Richard Giulianotti and Gary Armstrong argue that:

> '...academics have failed to examine adequately the spatial dimension underlying hooligan conflicts... The intensification of police control strategies has helped to engender a broadening of social spaces; contexts and techniques by which hooligans may 'legitimately' pursue confrontations. The concluding discussion critically assesses the effects and cultural meanings of increased police surveillance over football fans, noting the response of some hooligans in seeking to 'arrange' confrontations with rivals at extremely peripheral, non-football locations.'

Translated, this means that, having been pushed out of their regular arenas, those bent on conflict have consecrated new ones. This throws up an amusing parallel between Stoke City's naughty forty and those initiated into the peace-loving Wiccan tradition who place little emphasis on traditional holy sites. Instead, they make the venue they have chosen sacred through the calling of the four guardians and the placing of colours at the correct points of the compass. The naughty forty have a slightly different understanding of colours but would certainly appreciate the notion of guarding all points. Others in both the pagan and mainstream religious traditions are far more precious about venerable holy sites, from the standing stones and barrows of the megalithic priests or the groves of the Druids to other venerable gathering places, whether temple or common. The drawback is that if one side identifies a place as sacred, the other knows precisely where to target.

This desecration of a place revered by one's enemy is a theme that runs through all human societies, from the Romans cutting down the sacred groves of the Druids to Protestants' destruction of idols in the Reformation. The defilement of a holy place violated the sacredness of the site, which then had to be purified afterwards. There are regular newspaper reports of the 'satanic' desecration of churches, though on investigation the culprits often turn out to be rock fans who have over-indulged on cider. The point, though, is to wound (or at least insult) a perceived enemy.

As a boy, I saw a good example at the Stretford End after the last instalment of possibly the dullest final in history, the 1977 League Cup encounter between Everton and Aston Villa. A scoreless bore at Wembley was followed by a grim one-all after extra time at Hillsborough. The FA (which was beginning to regret its policy of replaying important games over and over) moved the second replay to Old Trafford. With only minutes of extra time to go, and final release through penalties for the first time in an English cup competition, a defensive error allowed Brian Little to pop up for Aston Villa's third and winning goal. Trudging out of Old Trafford, I noticed scrawled at the back of the terrace in huge letters, 'EFC agro'. Of course, the opportunity had been too good for the more atavistic element amongst the Everton support to miss – the hooligan equivalent of an open goal. I'm equally sure that the graffiti lasted about as long as it took the Mancunians to enter the stadium the following weekend. However, a point had been made, a sacred site violated.

Marking the place of your enemy is one thing but in the same year Scottish fans took matters a stage further and tore apart the pitch and nets at Wembley, taking it away along with anything else portable. The victorious Tartan hordes were keen on something more personal than a snowstorm of Piccadilly Circus, a souvenir of their visit that wasn't available from the club shop. Turf of the enemy unwillingly taken, as fellow Scot JK Rowling might have phrased it. No doubt this Caledonian mob saw themselves as quasi-mystical descendants of Bonnie Prince Charlie or Pictish raiders of a Saxon settlement. In a sense, they were bang on. More recently, *Scotland on Sunday* reported Scottish construction workers leaving a stash of Scots memorabilia including tartan scarves under the turf and dug outs of the new Wembley. Celtic and Scotland legend Billy McNeill commented that at least the prank 'will save us taking pieces of turf back home with us again'. There were other stories that construction workers from Middlesbrough placed Boro scarves in the new arch.

In occult circles, a sacrosanct spot might be a temple, a stone circle or just possibly a clearing in the woods used for meetings. Wembley, for example, derives its name from a pre-Norman Conquest meeting place in a clearing named after a man called Wemba. That Wembley should continue to attract the faithful centuries after the Germanic tribes who settled the area had moved on appears to be a happy coincidence. The conjunction of a revered meeting spot and the hallowed turf is perhaps to be expected, as football stadia or pitches are frequently referred to as shrines, sacred turf or holy ground. They are where people come to worship and where heroes do battle, and they develop their own myths. Many of the following tales are likely to be urban legends but the point is that, like any faith, people want to believe they are real. Or, as Michael Goss writing in the *Fortean Times* ('Curse and Effect', October 1996) puts it:

> 'Fabricated fokelore or fakelore, ersatz traditions can become the genuine article if the folk, in this case the fans, decide to accept them as genuine. This will certainly happen if they go on retelling the story.'

Wembley itself owes a good deal of its prominence to the peculiar tale of the 'White Horse final'. It was the first FA Cup played at the Empire Stadium, and the over-capacity crowd spilled all over the pitch. To the rescue came a hero on a white charger called Billie who single-handedly, yet gently, eased the masses back beyond the touchlines so the game could take place. Aside from the connotations this has with knights and St. George and other heroes on white chargers, it taps straight into the ancient British cult of the white horse whose chalk effigy adorns the hillside at Uffington, Wiltshire. The white horse was the main sacrificial animal in northern mythology, used in divination and especially associated with the fertility goddess Freyr. It was also the type chosen by Lady Godiva on which to enter Coventry naked. Something happily not copied by the 1987 FA Cup winning team when they toured the city.

Football grounds across the country have usurped the traditional role of the church or temple. Aside from being places of worship, prayers and collective singing they can also be where devotees have their ashes scattered. The popularity of stadia as a fan's final resting place is raising some ethical issues and as teams move grounds, expect to hear ghost stories involving new flats haunted by the shades of rowdy supporters. Highbury has a head start here as it was already apparently host to the shade of former manager Herbert Chapman and a horse that died during the construction of the North Bank. These locations are sacrosanct to home fans. They are where rituals take place, tribal songs are sung and legends told and passed down the generations. They are where hopes, dreams and beliefs are expressed and, more often, dashed. Home supporters might take away souvenirs to cherish from their own theatre of dreams, whether from the official shop where merchandising is increasingly imaginative (the Emile

Heskey Native American Dream Catcher can't be long in coming, can it?), or less obviously commercial items such as ticket stubs.

That programmes or other ephemera carry power by association would come as no surprise to Wiccans as they have a strong belief in sympathetic magic, based on the notion that energy inhabits everything and that objects therefore have power. They would appreciate why grass and other features of the football ground have an almost fetishistic appeal to home supporters. They may however have been less willing than 5000 Arsenal fans were to pay £25 a pop for a square foot of Highbury turf, or bid for various fixtures and fittings when the team moved away in 2006. It is worth mentioning here the importance of a sense of place, which Arsenal, uniquely in English football, have lacked ever since they moved from Woolwich to Highbury in 1913. In a clever way around this, Gillespie Road tube station was renamed Arsenal, thereby 'creating' a home area if you like. Many supporters would regard the relics they took from Highbury as holy. It may well have actually been blessed – several teams have had their grounds hallowed and others have been linked to a church from their inception.

It is not just the established church that is involved in the consecration of sports stadia. There are also examples of pagan rituals, exorcisms and purifications. For Swansea City in 2001, this meant a voodoo dance by Kenyan tribal dancers. This was to lift the dark spirits of the Vetch Field that were causing a bad run of form and that some people believed had led to the suicide of 1920s star Tich Evans. Unfortunately evil won out and a heavy downpour (no doubt brought on by Cardiff-based necromancers) caused the ceremony to be postponed on account of the pitch being waterlogged.

They are not alone in being disappointed by the occult. When Leyton Orient employed a druid to lift a curse on Brisbane Road, Matt Simpson writing in The View From the North Terrace was predictably sardonic: 'And there we were thinking that it was a combination of bad management, poor performances and a shortage of decent strikers'. Oxford United asked a bishop to perform a ceremony at their new Kassam Stadium, though the bishop insists that it was a blessing, not an exorcism to lift a 'gypsy curse'. This is an urban legend also associated with Leeds United, Derby County, Gillingham, Manchester City, Preston North End and Birmingham City in which a group of travellers had to be evicted prior to the construction of each of the teams' stadia. In the case of Oxford, the club's chaplain, the Reverend

Michael Chantry, said the farmer who originally owned the land had allowed gypsies to stay in return for helping him with harvesting and haymaking. When the field was sold to the club, the gypsies were thrown out and cast the curse in retaliation.

In the Midlands, there are two possible origins of the curse at St. Andrews, the home of Birmingham City. The first is that it related to a girl being murdered and left on the site, the other that it was the Romanies again. Manager Ron Saunders is believed to have had the players' boots painted red and called in a priest. Later boss Barry Fry took a more radical approach after a local medium advised him to take a leak on the four corner flags on the stroke of midnight before the next home game. He followed her instructions and the next day the team strode out confidently (being careful where they put the ball during corners) only to be savaged four-nil by Wolves. After that result, there is no record as to whether the medium was ever paid for her services.

In South London, a disgruntled psychic ended up cursing the ground himself after he was called in to lay the ghost of Billy Callender, a former Crystal Palace goalkeeper who hanged himself in 1932. Carlisle United are another team to score an own goal after the council commissioned an art piece known as 'the Mother of all curses'. In a short space of time three people died in torrential rain, surrounding farmland was ravaged by foot and mouth, buildings were destroyed and Carlisle United were relegated. The contrite artist is quoted as saying. 'If I thought my sculpture would have affected one Carlisle United result, I'd have smashed it myself years ago.'

Derby County were more successful with clearing the spell on the Baseball Ground, their home for a century from 1895, though it took them a while to do anything about it. After moving in, there followed a run of unfortunate results including losing three FA Cup finals in 1898, 1899 and 1903, on the last occasion six-nil to Bury. A series of relegations and promotions followed without any cups (though they did record some strong finishes in the top division) until the 1945-1946 season, when they got to the final again. Determined to leave nothing to chance with this one, the players, led by their captain Jack Nicolas, went out of their way to ask the gypsies' descendants to lift the curse. Their appeal (there is no record of silver crossing palms) appeared to work because they beat Charlton Athletic four-one after extra time, to finally lift some proper silverware.

Leaving aside any latent anti-Romany prejudice, it could be argued that the gypsy curse is a kind of neutral event or response to a perceived injustice by non-footballing folk. It is unlikely, for example, that the gypsies were fans of Aston Villa or Nottingham Forest and wished to punish local rivals. That didn't stop an attempt by Birmingham fans to lift the curse by transferring masonry from St. Andrews to Villa Park when both grounds were undergoing building work. This is in keeping with modern urban legends that could very much be viewed as 'enemy action'. It is also fair to assume that we can expect more of this sort of activity as teams leave traditional homelands and build new grounds on fresh sites.

The most common example of cursing or spoiling the site is the burial of the opposing team's shirts underneath the ground. This is simple sympathetic magic, whereby objects are believed to store energy and crucially interfere with the ambience of a place. Then again, building sports stadia on a Saxon burial ground could just be considered careless. Southampton had a terrible start to the 2001 season at St. Mary's, the replacement for the tight, intimidating Dell. Someone raised the possibility that the boneyard on which it was built might be to blame, so a pagan priestess was brought in to bless the ground. Cerridwen 'Dragonoak' Connelly conducted the ceremony outside St. Mary's and is quoted as saying:

> 'The Saxons loved gatherings and competitions and I am sure they were the kind of people who would be delighted for a stadium like this to be built over their remains. The players should see it in that light and see it as something positive. Saxons, it is good to have you here and the players want to celebrate this and accept that this is also your home. I predict Saints will beat Charlton.'

She was correct – Southampton won one-nil against a team, ironically, named after a former Saxon village. Rumours of a curse persisted, however, but these had little to do with ancient Saxons and a lot to do with modern Portsmouth, whose fans are said to have buried three shirts under the pitch during the construction of the new stadium. There is no doubt that some of the builders were from Portsmouth but official Portsmouth supporters organisations dismiss this, along with other tales that Pompey fans inscribed bricks in the foundations and even planted seeds in the centre circle, which will eventually sprout to spell the word 'Pompey'. There was one other place on the south coast where an ancient site and football ground coexisted, Brighton and Hove Albion's former Goldstone Ground. The Goldstone itself though was moved from the site of the stadium to a nearby park where it still stands.

There are always natural fears as teams and fans leave their spiritual home and settle into a new environment. Arsenal's record at their new stadium in 2007 was patchy, unbeaten for most of the season but lots of games drawn that might have been won at Highbury. Still, their form was good enough to stop rumours of Spurs fans sabotaging the place but the supporters in their temple were confused as they tried to replicate the certainties of the old ground. This was best summed up by rival sets of Arsenal devotees at opposite ends of the Emirates ground. One lot had a picture of a clock on a flag draped over the upper tier; the other a banner reading 'this is the Clock End'. Both groups were trying to recreate the area behind the goal nearest the away fans at Highbury. On a more recent visit, this appeared to have been sorted but to pretend, even now in these days of corporate boxes, that football stadia are just bricks and mortar is to miss the point. However much the grandeur and local colour is diminished by calling a stadium after a daps manufacturer (Bolton) or christening a stand 'the Text 64446 End' (Walsall) they are still great emotional, spiritual hubs and centres of identity as well as places of entertainment.

Mario Benedetti, a Uruguayan writer, put it rather well when he suggested that 'the stadium is the skeleton of a crowd' and can hide some strange secrets. In Zambia Profound Warriors FC seemingly magic unbeaten home run came to an end when opponents started changing in the car park and entering the ground through the spectators entrance rather than the one reserved for the away team. Coincidence or not the spell was broken. Across the ocean in Brazil the twelve year curse of Arubinha's frog caused Vasco da Gama to dig up their entire pitch with a tractor after a frog was allegedly buried under it. The amphibian was to emphasise the curse which Arubina invoked after he thought da Gama had unsportingly thrashed his team 12-0. In the end the curse fell one year short but eleven trophyless years was considered an extreme punishment for a club of Da Gama's stature and since then they have employed their own 'priest' to take care of such matters. Corinthians went even longer, twenty two years, without a championship, before they called in a crack team of spiritualists to their ground where, aside from conducting a lengthy ceremony, they dug up human teeth and femur, as well as the remains of a frog.

Over the border in Argentina, Boca Juniors fans arrive with live chickens to slaughter as a means of taunting supporters of River Plate. Another great Argentine derby is between Club Atlético Independiente and Racing (pronounced RAH-sing), both from the Buenos Aires suburb of Avellaneda. In the 1960s Independiente fans buried seven cat corpses beneath the Juan Domingo Peron Stadium that Racing officials failed to find the last of until 2001. Racing won the championship the following year for the first time since the 1960s. Just before that (in 1998) Racing were threatened with bankruptcy and the fans enthusiastically joined in with a ceremony at their stadium designed to exorcise the club's demons. Racing club president at the time Daniel Lalin claimed that: 'We are uniting Roman Catholicism with Racingism. It is an act of faith. The same faith displayed by the fans who stoically go to the stadium every Sunday.'

The ceremony included a Mass, complete with a priestly blessing of the team and the goals, whilst a choir sang Handel's Messiah. The service continued with a rock concert by local band Vox Dei (The Voice of God) and a banner was hung from the stands that read: 'God is a Racing fan. The devil is not'. This was a dig at Independiente, whose nickname is the Red Devils. All this was very lovely but Racing actually lost their next game two-nil. Nevertheless, overall it appeared to work because the government, in the form of the president, bailed out Racing and their stadium, on the grounds that they were part of the national heritage.

That could be construed as a kind of magic but the Racing club president hit on a very important point, the faith of the fans. They are an essential part of a place and whilst a ground, or indeed a cathedral, can be impressive empty, it is often the imprint of people that has made them so. Sometimes, though, a stadium can exist without a team, as happened in 1892 when Liverpool FC was created because Everton had left Anfield after a dispute with the landlord. A similar situation occurred in West London when Fulham refused to use the Stamford Bridge racing track, preferring their Cottage on the Thames. Again faced with an empty stadium, a team (London FC, though happily they ended up being the more modest Chelsea FC) was found to fill it, a clear case of nature abhorring a vacuum. Or the devil finding work for idle hands.

If a story reported in the *Guardian* (10 July 2004) is to be believed then Chelsea might have had an even closer association with the dark side. This suggested that Britain's leading occultist, the self styled beast of revelation and wickedest man in the world, Alistair Crowley, not only chose the colour of Chelsea's shirt but also aligned the pitch using dark forces in 1905. Sadly, all the evidence is circumstantial. Crowley did live in Chelsea but not until the 1930s, which was three decades after Chelsea FC moved in and way after the shirt colour changed from the lighter blue racing colours of the Earl of Cadogan to the current shade in 1912.

Many archetypal evil characters in twentieth century film and literature were based on Crowley. He crops up in stories by Ian Fleming (Casino Royale), Somerset Maugham (the Magician) and MR James (Casting the Runes, filmed as Night of the Demon), several Dennis Wheatley books and virtually any programme in which a sinister bald man with a goatee appears, except Match of the Day. He is supposed to have summoned a demon in the North African desert and, even more disturbingly, aligned several golf courses using occult energies. It is these same powers that he allegedly brought to bear at the Bridge in summoning up the points of the compass (East, South, West and North, to put them in correct magic order) and their corresponding spirits and energies. This, at least, is one tradition that was kept up until recently by Chelsea fans who sang 'We are the east side, we are the east side we are the east side of the Shed, We are the west side etc'.

A recent Chelsea manager, Jose Mourinho, appreciated what a full and vibrant stadium could achieve when he said 'I felt the power of Anfield, it was magnificent.' He also said many less complimentary things about Liverpool and their ground and supporters but he probably won't be the last and certainly wasn't the first to note the effect of the atmosphere. The fact is that Shankly Gates is a point of pilgrimage for people from all over the world, a religious totem that, since the Hillsborough disaster of 1989, carries extra potency as a memorial site to the victims. Less well known is that one hundred years previously the then tenants Everton installed the mast of a cursed ship, the Great Eastern, as the flagpole at the Kop End where it still stands.

Powerful magic (or, if you prefer, psychology) also lies behind the famous 'This is Anfield' sign in the tunnel. It serves to remind the Liverpool team of the place, its history and its sense of tradition. Bill Shankly also recognised that such a sign would spur a great player on and make them play better against Liverpool but would intimidate lesser ones. He correctly surmised that there are a lot more average players than greats about and that the sign, which the home team touches every time they pass it, would work in Liverpool's favour. By the 1960s such tactics were becoming necessary as due to improving standards the top grounds were becoming more alike, at least in terms of pitch quality. Although football pitches can vary in length and width, slopes, dips and strange wind patterns caused by gaps in stands are less common than in the past. One result has been a drop in the percentage of games ending in home wins from fifty seven percent in the early twentieth century to forty five by the twenty-first.

Improvements in travel and the curtailing of the most intimidating aspects of an away trip have not entirely removed the advantage. In fact what is surprising given the disparities in team's strengths even between sides in the same division is how strong home advantage remains. The win statistics above do not tell the full story because home advantage can also manifest itself by a weaker team getting a draw at home in a match they would have lost away. On this criteria home teams took about seventy percent of the points up to World War Two when it dropped to sixty where it remains. The reason it appears is tribal, a raising of testosterone levels amongst home players defending their patch against invaders and interestingly this is true of foreign as much as local ones as Celtic's home record in the Champions League shows.

Southern teams, and in particular fancy foreign players, are famously fearful of a cold night in Hartlepool or Grimsby and even in the Premiership, violent incidents against opposing players are not unknown. However, it is other, less intimidating aspects of fan behaviour that are more popularly believed to get results. It has become a cliché to hear commentators say that the Stretford End is worth five minutes injury time to Manchester United, that Ipswich's fearsome North Standers can suck the ball into the net, and all manner of other magical things. Fans, players and commentators enjoy this myth but there is little evidence to back it up. It is true that a passionate, heavily partisan crowd can unsettle visiting players and lift home ones but in terms of influencing the result it may be the officials who are affected the most.

One study examined the influence of crowd sounds on decisions by showing recordings of games to similarly experienced officials some with the sound included and some without. Those with the crowd noises were consistently less certain in their decision making and, more crucially, awarded more decisions in favour of the home team.

To fans though the real magic of stadia are the tribal memories and collective beliefs. The way a whisper can start at the Gallowgate End Newcastle only to be taken up by thousands in a mighty chorus, or the seething hostility of the New Den, all give soul to bricks and mortar. A sense of place, belief, shared hopes and dreams will inevitably leave some imprint from the past on the present or, as a medium might suggest, such places have vibrations, at least to those visiting them.

Vibrations, concepts of the past, ghosts and demons are all ridiculous, surely, when it comes down to the most important thing about football: money? The financial implications are what made it vital for the sake of the whole of English football to lift the 'south-side spell' at the Millennium Stadium in Cardiff. Several teams had expressed unease, and more importantly lost, after using the southern dressing room at the stadium in Cardiff, which until 2007 stood in for Wembley as the venue for England's domestic cup finals and play offs. A feng shui expert was brought in to alter the energy of the room by scattering incense and sea salt, lighting candles and chanting. As part of a belt and braces approach, Cerridwen Connelly, by now quite the expert at ground counter-cursing, was asked to bless the stadium. Whatever they did worked in 2002, when Stoke City used the changing room on their way to winning promotion. Of course, none of this matters so much now that English football has returned to its spiritual home at Wembley.

That phrase easily trips off the tongue, or even the word processor, but there is absolutely no reason why Wembley should be the spiritual home of anything in the twentieth century and beyond. The Football Association had wanted a neutral venue for the cup final and Wembley hadn't been the front runner. It was built in ten months in 1922, greyhound racing was a bigger earner than football in its early years and subsequently speedway, rugby league, horse shows and rock concerts have all contributed to its upkeep. Potential rivals like Stamford Bridge, White City near Shepherds Bush (which predated Wembley and was used in both the 1908 Olympics and 1966 World Cup), Crystal Palace and the Oval had equally strong claims, better locations and larger capacities, as well as a history of holding finals.

The stadium suffered the so called 'Wembley hoodoo' in the 1950s after a series of high profile injuries including Elton John's uncle (Roy

Dwight) breaking his leg in a cup final. These were really more to do with the unavailability of substitutes, so players carried on way beyond the time they might today. It was in the 1950s that another great cup final (the Matthews one) settled Wembley's position – that and the media. In a religious sense, Wembley is a TV evangelist success story. In the distant days of limited football on television, it was likely to be the only ground that most football fans saw, other than their own, and in comparison to virtually all other stadia in the country it shone out. So alongside the football itself came the daft banners, stupid jokes and eulogies to the great stadium and the games played there. It became a place of pilgrimage, a Mecca, which finally delivered its own miracle in 1966 with the whole world watching. Places do not have to be ancient or holy to be magic – people can make a place sacred through their faith, rituals and belief. Wembley has come a long way from being a Saxon clearing in the woods, even if it's still a place in which Germanic tribes occasionally meet to do battle.

Blue is the colour
Shirts and colours

There are parts of the world where wearing the wrong kit can get you killed. Obviously this is true of war zones, but it's also the case of those urban areas in the Americas where colours signify different gangs. This identification with a colour operates on many levels, from the practical to the psychological and even the spiritual. Some of the reasoning behind the design and hue of military uniforms, for example, is similar to the considerations that a sports club might contemplate when choosing a strip. This was more obviously apparent in past times, such as the Vikings who wore interesting and threatening headgear on their forays in search of European silverware. Another case in point is the brilliant red coat that was sported by Britain's empire boys. To the modern military mind, wearing a colour that stands out so clearly might be considered suicidal on the battlefield; but, aside from its cultural associations, a red tunic has the advantage of not revealing the blood that has been shed on it. The idea was to parade a force that was smartly turned out, courageously did not hide on the battlefield and, because it was hard to see whether a soldier was wounded and bleeding, appeared to be invincible.

Not all of these virtues can be transferred to the football pitch where, on occasion, feigning injury can work to a player's advantage but there is an entire industry based on the psychology and healing properties of different colours. IBM computers and Barclays Bank use blue to suggest calmness and order in their branding, and different shades have been associated with virtue or vice, health or illness for centuries and give rise to phrases like 'seeing red' or 'looking a bit green'. In the home people say things like: 'A burnt Tuscan orange would make the room warmer' and folk may nod sagely around the coffee table when discussing a friend's deplorable colour combinations and whisper in hushed tones: 'Chocolate brown with double virtual stripes? Who told them that was a good idea?'

Leaving aside Coventry City's 1970s away strip, most people have instinctive or acquired knowledge of what works well and looks good on them, and of classic fashion fiascos such as it being unwise for ginger-haired people to wear pink or plump people to wear hoops. The veracity of the latter will, of course, be plain to anyone familiar with Kevin Gallen's playing career at QPR. Portsmouth aside, the ginger hair and pink combination has not really been tested recently, although pale pink does crop up in various away strips, when it is often disguised as 'washed salmon' or some other Dulux-inspired euphemism. This was less true in the early days of the League when many teams, including Bolton, Stockport and (perhaps ironically, given their nickname) West Ham, played in pink. People laughed at Coventry City in the 1970s, but brown was a surprisingly popular colour in the earlier part of the twentieth century, with Leicester, Mansfield, Barnsley and Grimsby among the teams sporting various shades of it. West Brom (in the days when they were known as the West Bromwich Strollers) took the candy box motif to its logical conclusion by topping off their blue and chocolate ensemble with a pompom hat.

In terms of the colour of their shirts, which are royal blue with some red detail, psychologist Angela Wright thinks the French have it right when it comes to football. She explains:

> 'Blue is the colour of the mind, and may work to 'psyche out' their opponents as it suggests they will play a well thought out and strategic game. This thoughtful colour, combined with the aggression and power of red, achieves a great balance as it conveys that the team has both brains and brawn.'

Ms Wright also rates the red and gold of Spain, as the physical presence of the red complements the warm yellow and oozes confidence. Anyone sceptical about such 'readings' of colour might do well to consider her scarily appropriate analysis of the Dutch's orange tops; despite knowing nothing about football, she reveals they suggest to her a boisterous and talented team, but one that is also disorganised.

Psychologically then colours have meaning but for those involved in the occult colour really is a language with energy and power. For example, black is the preferred choice for Wiccans, as it absorbs all colours and can take on anything. In this tradition, colours are linked to a whole array of other things, such as planets, each with their own specific attributes and associations. So the most popular colour for teams in England and Scotland, blue, is used to induce the power of Saturn and water. It represents, amongst other things, tranquillity, strength, opportunity and wealth, and should, if worn in the right combination, imbue its wearer with one or more of these characteristics.

The English League's next most popular colour, red, has altogether fierier and more aggressive associations. It draws on aspects of Mars such as power and strength, as well as being invigorating and passionate. According to colour therapists, red is ideally suited to sports, which might explain why in England red teams win more than blue overall, or indeed why England won the World Cup playing in red rather than their traditional white. Some teams like to balance their colours by using contrasts on the shorts or socks, and Liverpool's all-red look is a deliberate contrast to Manchester United's white shorts and use of black in their socks. By doing this, Liverpool make the statement that they are the true reds. Along with Arsenal, these are the three most consistently successful teams. In fourth place is the top blue side, Everton, and in fifth place is one of the few teams who play in claret, Aston Villa. Leading white-shirted teams include Preston North End, Tottenham Hotspur, Derby County and Leeds United. The colour white (which is the third most popular colour in England and second in Scotland) is associated in one tradition with the moon and is good for clarity, calming doubts, peace and truth. In tarot though the moon is linked to the unconscious and howling dogs. So – Bolton Wanderers all over, really.

White was one of the four colours used by the chariot-racing teams in Ancient Rome, the others being green and those great rivals the reds and the blues. The passion and violence still remains today, though when Roma (red) play Lazio (blue), it is thankfully at a much lower level. Green has rather dropped off the scene in English football, with the exception of goalkeepers and referees. During the Middle Ages, green was used to symbolise Satan, it is also associated with Islam and pre-Christian cults such as the Green Man. The fact that football shares its roots with exactly the sort of pagan gatherings that celebrated Jack in the Green and other folk festivals should have made green a more popular colour. In England, however, it was adopted by few sides outside Plymouth in the agricultural south-west, although Exeter and Bristol Rovers both flirted with it. To confuse the issue further, in Scotland, the green strips of Celtic and Hibernian reach out to their original support base, the (predominantly Catholic) immigrant Irish population. In the Scottish game, religion plays a much more obvious role in the choice of kit colour than it does for the English. North of the border teams with Presbyterian roots are more likely to play in red, white or blue (the colours of the Union Flag).

Chesterfield, the only team to appropriate the flag itself as a kit, did so briefly in 1892, just as rules on standard kits were being brought in. At that time, the jersey (as it was known) would not have stood out quite so noticeably against the many halved, quartered and hooped tops of the period. Some teams took their designs from rugby clubs, and others from racing colours linked to the heraldic past of the owners or the municipality. There was an awful lot of experimentation and swapping about, with many teams literally playing the colour field and Burnley winning the prize for the most extreme changes. It might be best to whisper this in some quarters, but both Tottenham and Newcastle dallied with red, while Liverpool once wore blue and white squares. Over time, practical issues such as cost, availability of dyes and the standards imposed by the League structure tended to weed out the more exotic tops. Blackburn Rovers, almost uniquely, remain true to their original jersey to this day, in both pattern and colour.

Away kits give clubs an opportunity to remind their supporters of their history, suggest a broader identity and associate with other, perhaps classier teams. Newcastle United started the trend of playing in a yellow away shirt in honour of Brazil. Other examples of English dreaming include Blackpool's orange (though they insist on calling it 'tangerine') after Holland, and Derby's pioneering use of the light blue of Argentina as their spare kit. The reserve jersey, today little more than a marketing opportunity, could once be seen as a more experimental, cavalier side to a team's character, while its main colour stressed its core identity.

One of the problems with colour identity and the spiritual world is that they are culturally dependent, and therefore differ across the globe. In the East white is the colour associated with death rather than black, as it is in the West. In Asia, yellow is the royal colour and purple is used for widows' mourning whereas in Europe, purple is regal and yellow aligns with sunny optimism, cowardice and madness. Sometimes, colours even have conflicting meanings within cultures, so black, for example, can mean rebellion and conformity as well as death. Hull, Derby and Manchester City all had black tops once, despite it being a colour commonly associated with the dark arts or black magic. Black was actually banned as a strip colour for much of the twentieth century when it was appropriated by the occasional real devils of the field, the officials.

In footballing terms, black is rarely used today except in combination with its magical opposite, white. Whether this means that Grimsby Town are trying to emulate William Blake in some sort of marriage of heaven and hell is open to conjecture. In *The Soccer Tribe*, Desmond Morris suggests that colours carry with them associations of a previous era and that the popularity of white in England is due to it being the colour of supposed racial superiority. The supremacy of the colour white in late Victorian England was based not only on the ascendancy of the white nations but also on the colour's association with honourable virtues and positive thoughts, in contrast to 'black moods' and 'black hearted villains' or people being 'blackballed'. All this is quaint and faintly laughable in today's game, where many of the exceptional black and mixed race players play in white tops.

The past has an echo, though, which explains the enduring popularity of white shirts and does make sense psychologically. Many people believe that success rubs off and accordingly choose to be allied with triumphant teams. White has associations of innocence and purity, but also conjures up the image of the hero on a white charger. This is not why Tottenham Hotspur play in white, however; there is no link back to Sir Henry (Harry Hotspur) Percy (1366-1403). The real reason is that it is a tribute to the great Preston North End team of 1900. Real Madrid copied the top amateur side of an earlier era, the Corinthians, who were noted for their sense of fair play. It might be best not to mention that to Leeds, who dropped their blue and yellow strip in favour of white in honour of the Spanish side in the late 1950s. Quite what Juventus were thinking of when they adopted the black and white Notts County outfit is harder to assess, though perhaps it's no stranger than cross town rivals Nottingham Forest electing to wear the Garibaldi red in honour of the Italian revolutionary.

Colour choice is also meant to lend a team some sort of psychological advantage over rivals. Bright colours not only make team-mates easier to spot but also signal that the wearer is proud and fearless: the stronger the colour the fiercer the wearer. On a strictly practical level, colours carry important messages about their teams. The wearers look conspicuous on the field and contrast with both their immediate opponents and their neighbouring rivals. Choice is somewhat dictated by others. One cannot have the same colour as a local antagonist, so Sheffield Wednesday play in blue and Sheffield United in red. In London, this issue did not arise until relatively recently because teams playing in the same colour were in different divisions, so Arsenal's red or Tottenham's white did not collide with those of (respectively) Charlton or Brentford, Fulham or Orient. Fulham and Charlton's stints in the top division have rather confused things but generally the pattern holds.

This would never be an issue if the idea that Liverpool FC proposed in 1904 had been adopted. They suggested that, in Football League games, all home teams should wear red and the visitors white, which would have taken most of the colour and a good deal of the symbolism from the game. As it is, one side must change to a different strip when two similarly coloured sides clash; until 1921, it was the home side that switched. In more sporting Scotland, this was the case until the 1990s. By this time, most English sides had introduced a third strip to their colour palette, usually one that bore no relation to their regular strip. This resulted in shades of yellows and pale blues unseen at soccer grounds since the colourful Victorians.

Whatever the pattern or tint of top, one of the most damning chants in football is when fans tell their team they are not fit to wear the shirt. The shirt, tribal insignia and badge carry important associations and are the direct descendants of the heraldic banners – magic flags – of other eras. In this context, footballers take on the mantle of tribal champions, representatives of a philosophy, region or way of life. The wearing of the shirt or adoption of colours symbolises, to the faithful, a kind of mystical sense of belonging and identity that holds true from teen gang members to the 'ghost shirts' worn by the Teton Sioux. In each case, the clothing and colour imbues the wearer with extra power by association, and it is this that football clubs try to inspire by their colour choices. Just like the ghost shirts, which were supposed to make their wearers invulnerable to bullets, however, colour does not have a magical ability to attract or repel the ball; it can only psychologically inspire the wearer to greater feats.

That psychological inspiration can be enough to affect outcomes. According to anthologists working at Durham University red is consistently associated with a higher probability of winning, they even suggested that this might be genetically predetermined. In a different study goalkeepers were asked to rate penalty takers on likely competence (based on things like composure and confidence) and also their own likelihood of saving a kick. Those wearing red were rated more highly and the keeper's confidence, and therefore probability, of saving from ones wearing other colours was higher. Sometimes colours or flags were rallying points or designed to terrify opponents. Sometimes they promised protection as when members of the Highlands and Islands regiment carried pieces of a 'Fairy Banner' in their pockets for luck in World War One. The armies that marched under the original Fairy Banner had never been defeated but by then it was too delicate to be taken into war in its entirety.

Wear and tear was not the reason for relatively recent dramatic identity rebrandings at Coventry, Oldham and others. When teams experiment across the colour spectrum nowadays, it tends to be for commercial reasons – re-issues of 'classic' away strips, for example, or ones that'll look good with jeans. Manchester United famously fell foul of this trend when they elected to play in their 'third' away strip in a match against Southampton. As well as losing, they inspired a whole series of popular football books called *The Wrong Kind of Shirt*. The tops were grey, thus failing to meet two of the key criteria when it comes to a football strip: that it should make the team stand out and be proud of their bright plumage, and that it should enable them to see, recognise and pass to their team mates easily. The grey strip failed on all levels – at least, that was the excuse given after the match – and it certainly fits the orthodox theories of colour and their meanings.

The huge commercial expansion of the game has blurred, to some extent, the simple colour patterns that had evolved since Victorian times. As football magazine *When Saturday Comes* wryly observed, fans of Aston Villa recently witnessed a combination (brought about by the sponsor's logo) uniting blue, claret, lime green and purple 'rarely seen outside of an infant school art class'. At the other extreme Barcelona, who kept their strips free of advertising longer than anyone else, still refuse to admit any white on the shirt because it is the colour of rivals Real Madrid. Elsewhere, the best way of telling a Spurs shirt from a Fulham one is not the cut or style, and obviously not the colour, but the sponsor. Then again, in terms of symbolism this is as good an indicator as any in the modern commercial world of a club's power and prestige – does their strip boast a household name or the slogan of a local cash and carry?

The point is that symbols and colours carry great power. They are rooted in humanity's past and tap into the need for belonging and identity. It is an important decision to make, so important that directors of top Argentine side Boca could not agree. In the end they compromised on the suggestion that they would adopt the colours of the next ship that arrived in Buenos Aires harbour, it happened to be Swedish. From this random beginning came one of the fiercest identifications with colour and emblem in the game. Argentine writer Osvaldo Soriano quotes the case of a Boca fan who was on his death bed. The supporter in question asked at the last moment for the yellow and blue of Boca to be removed and he be covered in the flag of rivals River Plate so that, with his own final breath, he could celebrate the death of 'one of them'.

Duncan is our hero
Crests and mascots

That (slightly bowdlerised) terrace tribute to Duncan Ferguson recognises that he was something of a rarity: a top flight footballer with clear tribal loyalties, who went as far as to have his adopted team crest tattooed on his arm. Of course, there are many footballers with tattoos. They range from traditional inscriptions of names to significant numbers (Fernando Torres), animals, Christian symbolism, angels, Aztec warriors (Harry Kewell) and Daniel Agger's various tribal markings. Others have inspirational slogans, such as Wayne Rooney who has 'just enough education to perform' on his right arm. There is probably a whole book to be written on pagan symbolism in sportsmen's tattoos, if anyone could be bothered to write it. However intricate the Hindu or Chinese calligraphy that adorns these athletes, in terms of power and a modern sense of belonging they are nothing beside the erect tower with wreaths resplendent (or picture of an old prison from Liverpool Five) on Duncan's arm.

Symbols carry power and meaning and, as well as expressing their allegiances, it is this that tattooed players are tapping into. In these times of rapid transfers and uncertainty, most of them opt for ancient runes or recent family arrivals, preferring to let their childhood teams and dreams fluctuate with each transfer window. In retirement, they can enjoy jocular rivalry in the media about their true footballing loves without fear of diminishing their own commercial value. For the fan, though, the club crest or logo is a tribal totem, something to protect and cherish and often accompanied by the only bit of Latin the average football supporter knows. This text follows a tradition that has its roots in academia and family dynasties, and bestows a certain gravitas and faux history to what are, after all, relatively modern institutions. The mottos often sound impressive, offer ideals to aspire to and, just possibly, by being written in a language not widely spoken for more than a millennium, limit satire.

Amongst the teams with a Latin motto are Sunderland (Consectatio Excellentiae, in pursuit of excellence), Plymouth (Semper Fidelis always faithful), Tranmere Rovers (Ubi fides ibi lux et robur, where there is faith, there is light and strength) and Bury (Vincit Omnia Industria, hard work overcomes everything). Some are more apt than others with traditionally robust Blackburn Rovers sporting Arte et labore (by skill and labour), lower league Scottish outfit Queens Park wear ludere causa lundendi (to play for the sake of the game) whilst Manchester City relish superbia in praelia or pride in battle. On a spiritual level there is Bristol City's Vim promovit insatum (promoting inner power) whilst Gillingham proclaims to be Domus clamantium or home of the shouting men.

For Queen's Park the motto is particularly relevant as they are the only amateur side in the Scottish League, yet play in one of the largest grounds in the country (Hampden Park). They are the oldest club in Scotland and have done wondrous things, including supplying all the players for the first ever international against England and the national strip of dark blue. They have played in two English FA Cup Finals (losing both times) and popularised the game throughout the (largely working class) central belt of Scotland, before helping to set up the Scottish FA in 1873. They also campaigned for the key rule change that allowed the ball to be passed forward in Association Football. No need for them to invent tradition – they are tradition, and have done much for the sake of the game.

Certain sides lifted their motto from the coat of arms of their county or town (this was the case for several of the early club crests and even colours as well) meaning that they took on the emblems of the community they were based in and helped establish a regional identity. These crests are the ones that have changed most over the years as clubs have evolved a unique character separate from, but rooted in, a given community. With an eye to the international appeal of symbols, these have been simplified or even completely transformed over time into a single emblem. Mansfield Town's stag is one example, although international recognition probably wasn't the key concern there.

One of the fundamental staples of the team badge is the inclusion of an element that evokes a sense of place: Motherwell use an illustration of Ravenscraig Steelworks, even though it closed in the 1980s, and Barnsley had a miner. Another theme is the use of a symbolic item associated with the club's origins. Arsenal's cannon, for example, derives from their days as the Woolwich Arsenal. Also popular is the use of a bird or animal that will imbue the team with some of its characteristics and allow the two to become synonymous. Newcastle United are an interesting example of this; their nickname, The Magpies, aptly denotes their policy for years in the Premier League of nicking players from everywhere, only to hoard them uselessly.

Popular creatures tend to be fierce hunters such as tigers or birds of prey, or majestic or powerful animals, like rams, bulls or stags. How these beasts are presented is another matter entirely; some are stylised, some are heraldic and others are more naturalistic. Lions feature on over a dozen crests but there is all the difference in the world between the slightly cross Macclesfield cat scarpering with some corn, and the pouncing beast of Millwall. Villa and Middlesbrough both have variations on the heraldic lion while Shrewsbury Town have a rather exhausted looking feline that might better be suited to pantomime or a tin of syrup. Realistic looking creatures feature for Hull (a tiger) and Hereford (a bull) but Derby's ram, Sheffield Wednesday's owl and, in particular, Swansea's swan are much more stylised. In all of these cases, the transference of strength, nobility, grace, wisdom or hunting prowess are suggested through the badges, while the heraldic symbolism of some them hints at a distant noble past which, at least in the case of Aston Villa, would be accurate. As would Ipswich's painfully candid badge which features a carthorse kicking a football which could mean an honest hardworking side from a rural area or could just suggest, well, carthorses kicking footballs.

At least Ipswich have a decent grasp of who they are which is questionable for the teams represented by mythical beings. There are a dozen of these from Aldershot Town's (appropriate) use of the phoenix to Lincoln City's imps via any number of griffins, dragons, unicorns and flying horses to the interesting lamb and flag Knights Templar motif used by Preston North End. Preston are rare in having such an overtly religious emblem and one which has no clear link to the place but an awful lot to freemasonry and mystical Christian cults arising from the crusades. The same could be said for Portsmouth whose Islamic looking gold star and crescent derives from the time of Richard the Lionheart but the motto 'heaven's light our guide' might be useful for a team with nautical connections. Many other sides use symbols more readily associated with their base community such as a ship on Plymouth Argyle's or the shrimp on Southend's badge which is the only use made of a fish in English professional football.

The wolf of Wolves and Nottingham Forest's forest are slight anomalies in that they clearly derive from the team's name, although both still make for easily recognised emblems. Nicknames or crests based on strip colour are more common, such as The Bluebirds of Cardiff City. For The Canaries of Norwich City, the pattern was reversed. The nickname came first as the place was famed for breeding canaries and they once played in an old quarry called The Nest so the yellow strip was adopted to fit that. When their previous nickname, The Rokerites, became obsolete after they moved their stadium, Sunderland chose The Black Cats after the Black Cat Battery that existed on the River Wear during the Napoleonic War – another example of local circumstances inspiring a nickname. For most of the reasons listed above, The Black Cats is a far better name, in both branding and occult terms (not to mention pictorial representation) than another of their nicknames, The Mackems, derived from the distant past when there was shipbuilding on the Wear.

Together with the deindustrialisation of Britain, such rebranding has had a widespread effect on club nicknames, and not all to the good. The traditional ones accurately portrayed how the industries of England were distributed with The Hatters (Luton and Stockport), The Cobblers (Northampton Town), The Saddlers (Walsall), The Railwaymen (Crewe Alexandra) and The Glovers (Yeovil Town). So far, teams have avoided reflecting the worst excesses of the new economic climate, which might have led to The Call Centre Operatives (Tranmere), The Ring Road Retailers (Bolton) or The Silicon Superheroes (Reading). Reading were once known as The Biscuitmen, though. This was nothing to do with going to pieces outside the box but, perhaps unsurprisingly, they now prefer to be known as The Royals, just as Chelsea ditched The Pensioners to become The Blues, and Crystal Palace The Glaziers to become The Eagles.

This last example is interesting in that it allegedly came about through fan power (or rather, a rich fan's power). The story goes that, in the 1980s, future Palace chairman and several hundred of his closest friends popped down to Brighton to take in the sea air and watch Palace tackle rivals Brighton and Hove Albion (The Seagulls). During the traditional pre-match sing along, the visitors shouted 'Eagles, Eagles' as a riposte to the locals' chant of 'Seagulls, Seagulls'.

Palace's South London rivals Charlton have shifted their nickname fairly regularly, dropping The Robins in favour of The Valiants, a reference to their ground (the Valley) and, latterly and rather obscurely, The Addicks, which is apparently how they say haddock in London SE7. Wrexham, who were also known as The Robins, swapped to the more dramatic Dragons, although several sides including Swindon seem happy to be named after the redbreast. One relatively late arrival to the nickname business are the Red Devils of Manchester United. They filched the name in the 1950s from rugby league team the Salford Reds, who earned it after a particularly ferocious tour of France.

Today, traditional 'virtues' such as ferocity and strength are often promoted by displaying weapons on the crest. Again, some of these are borrowed from heraldry or a place's distant past, while others suggest more recent events. Swords feature on the crests of Charlton (though these could be fish knives) and Sheffield United (reflecting the city's steel industry). There is a Viking on Doncaster Rovers' badge and, of course, there are the happy hammers of West Ham. This is not a derivation from the club name but because The Irons began as a team from an ironworks. It's a shame that Coventry City, who started life as a Singers sewing machine factory side, didn't stick to their roots in a similar fashion. It would have been worth it for the chants alone ('Sing with a singer, we only sing with a singer...'). Instead, they opted for The Skyblues and join a host of other sides whose colour is their pet name.

At various points, Leeds United have simply been The Whites or The Lilywhites, but they are perhaps the best example of a side with an identity crisis when it comes to crests and names and, for that matter, colour. In the 1970s, they changed their crest to a smiley face in an attempt to bury their reputation as 'ugly' Leeds. The idea was to realign the club by associating it with the 1960s counter culture, based on peace, love and harmony rather than pies, late tackles and harassment. To make them more Crosby, Stills, Nash and Young rather than, say, Clockwork Orange. This was not their first attempt at rebranding; they had already ditched the nickname The Peacocks, together with their Leeds City coat of arms featuring owls and the Latin motto Pro Rege et Lege (For King and the Law), in favour of a simple owl design. This was dropped in the 1960s, not because it clashed with both Oldham Athletic and Sheffield Wednesday, but because manager Don Revie thought all birds unlucky.

Don Revie almost deserves a chapter to himself, with his fear of birds and elephants, his ritual pre-match stroll to the traffic lights near Elland Road and his shiny lucky blue suit that had a certain 'tramp chic' in the later stages of his career. However, he managed to couple this old-world superstition with a very keen grasp of modern marketing and imagery, as well as fashioning a ruthlessly efficient side that won trophies. He always wanted Leeds to have an identity and something of the class of other successful teams. His first act was to change the strip from yellow and blue to white, in honour of Real Madrid (see the chapter on Colours) before turning to the crest. Together with Admiral Sportswear, he produced the first replica kit that could be sold to fans. This featured the smiley face logo but by the 1980s the peacock had returned, to be followed by various eye-catching permutations of the 'classic' LUFC script Revie had chosen to replace the owl. In 1994 came the white rose and ball badge (an attempt to create a broader pan-Yorkshire brand for the team using the symbol of the county), which, after sharing the shirt with the initials LUFC for a number of years, was abandoned. Revie's original LUFC script was back in time for Leeds' return to the lower divisions from which he'd led them decades before.

The smiley face is one of many disappearing icons including Manchester City's huge Maltese Cross and Heart of Midlothian in the pre-war period, resplendent in a strip that featured a big red heart. Leeds' former arch-rivals Chelsea seem to have settled with their branding. They were the first club to put their crest on a shirt, and altered their emblem from its original Chelsea Pensioner to the simple initials CFC onto a lion holding a staff, based on elements in the coat of arms of the Metropolitan Borough of Chelsea. The lion came from the arms of then club president Viscount Chelsea, and was apparently 'rampant regardant'; the staff was taken from the Abbots of Westminster, former Lords of the Manor of Chelsea. It also featured three red roses (to represent England) and two footballs. In the 1980s, a more relaxed lion hung above the CFC. This century, the heraldic lion was reinstated after fans complained the calm one was too similar (in appearance if not attitude) to Millwall's.

Such symbolic re-branding has rarely included the sort of imaginative American merging of name and nickname where teams are called New England Revolution or San Hose Eathquake. Where this has been done in rugby league in old England, it is uninspired and, worse, artificial. As a name, Leeds Rhinos simply does not work; to draw on the power of a particular beast, it should be related in some way to a local energy or source of pride as well, and rhinos are fairly rare in Headingley. Much better are locally inspired oddities, such as Bristol Rovers' nickname The Gas (supporters are known as Gasheads) in honour of a huge gas tower near one of their early homes; or Dundee United becoming dubbed The Arabs on account of them playing on sand because of the tendency of their pitch to become waterlogged.

These nicknames and crests, in occult terms, work through association and identity, with teams trying to summon up say the power (Crystal Palace) or nobility (Colchester) of an eagle. In sorcery circles, this is known as 'channelling', whereby the spirit of a creature is called upon to intercede, in this case, on behalf of a team. The idea of spirit animals is present in many belief systems and are a symbolic representation of the person (or team), who becomes or takes on some of the characteristics of a particular animal. The crest is the concentrated expression of the side – hence the annoying recent trend, amongst players wishing to express their devotion to the cause, of kissing the badge. However vexing it is for long term fans to see this misuse of the crest it is nothing to the fury of 120,000 Scots at Hampden Park when England international Alan Ball used the corner flag (bearing the Cross of St. Andrew) to blow his nose on in one international in 1972.

It is unclear whether clubs have a proper understanding of the occult significance of what their badges or nicknames are channelling (beyond a handy extra income stream) but, as with the planetary system that underpins much of western magic, so animals have very specific fields of influence – or pitches, if you will. By occult (and football) logic, Wrexham's Dragons are channelling wisdom and nobility, as well as suggesting a link to the land of their fathers. Sunderland's Black Cats tap into local history but also to the animal's spirit of independence and grace. The Foxes of Leicester City (formerly known as Leicester Fosse) hope to bring cunning and intelligence to their play with their foxy ways, Sheffield Wednesday's Owls offer wisdom and patience, and Derby County's Rams provide them with a new beginning. The swan gives Swansea balance, while the wolf head (again an ancient city emblem) provides Chester with attributes like loyalty and perseverance.

Should any team be looking to change their nickname, a few obvious suggestions leap to mind – the hummingbird (stopper of time) for Man United under Sir Alex Ferguson, perhaps, or the scorpion for any defensively minded team. Other appropriate symbols might be the yoyo, the dollar sign, the leaderless mob and the fallen giant.

Research into the clubs drew a blank response when they were asked whether they were adopting the totem animal shape-shifting tradition of European myth or the shamanistic power animal approach. Most of the workers in club shops quickly ended the conversation by saying something like: 'So are you interested in a bee-shaped pen or not?' (Brentford). Likewise, polite questions as to whether players visited the astral plane to engage with the clubs' totem before matches met with confused responses and directions to travel agents. That said, the ritual for contacting a spirit beast might not be unfamiliar to professionals preparing for a big match, involving as it does relaxing the body, clearing the mind, focusing on the task in hand and deep breathing, often accompanied by music. (See the chapter on Superstitions.) Doing this prepares you to face the wolves, whether spiritual or from Wolverhampton.

If the animal on the crest is fierce and aspirational, something to admire and call upon, its representation on the pitch in the form of mascot gives a nod to another pagan tradition. The pantomime beasts lurching along the touchline are truly Punch, kings for an afternoon (a rare exception was H'Angus the monkey at Hartlepool, who went on to be mayor of the town for two terms). In general, though, the vague sense of humiliation inherent to the role of mascot might explain why they are so prone to violent outbursts and obscene gestures. Cyril the Swan, Wolfie the Wolf and Bristol City's City Cat spring to mind here, along with Aston Villa's lion, who was fined for making improper advances to Miss Aston Villa. The appearance of whichever uber-ridiculous fan has disguised themselves as a mascot reassures the average supporter that they are not so badly obsessed that they need to don a poorly fitting animal suit and jog around like a loon. Only at Forfar (whose nickname is The Loons) might this be considered half way acceptable. In the occult world, this is known as drawing power. In terms of football marketing it's hard to say, but whoever in Stoke thought the Pottermus was a good idea should pray very hard for forgiveness.

The mascot is the holy fool of folklore, acting out and giving focus to the sense of the ridiculous possessed by all fans. The crest is the magic amulet or symbol of power. And the scarves, flags, shirts and other paraphernalia are the sacred robes of the chosen. Before occult rituals, symbols, clothes (often robes of prescribed colours) and instruments are carefully selected. In an interview for this book, one practising Wiccan guessed that for every thousand goth teenagers sporting pentagrams, only one will actually go on to be initiated to a coven. These are rather better odds than the shirt-wearing fan-to-player ratio, but the interviewee developed the analogy further and explained that, whereas the first pentagram would have been purchased, the second would have been bestowed, upon completion of an apprenticeship and often after years of doing relatively mundane assisting tasks. It would appear that the boot-approach has not been entirely lost to the world, even if it might be better renamed the broom-room.

Another key difference involves the choice of dates. In the world of the occult, these remain inviolate, dictated by tradition, ancient history, the phases of the moon and positions of the stars. In the world of football, the matter is more often driven by another extraterrestrial orbiting object, the satellite. This, often dangerous, disruption of game times comes alongside attempts to contain some of the more exuberant aspects of fan ritual and the proscribing of articles of worship. For example during the 2006 World Cup Dutch supporters were told to remove their orange tops because they sported an unofficial sponsor.

Oddly enough, the fetishism for flamboyant gestures on the one hand (such as wizard robes or team face paint) and miniscule symbols on the other (like the Masonic tiepin and the hooligan's designer logo) are further links between the two worlds. Replica-shirt-wearing followers and robe-donning occultists are the public faces of their respective tribes. But being able to read the runes of football clothing can be a very useful social skill. It can mean the difference, say, between staying in the pub for a nice drink and running before its windows are smashed. Hooligan fashion 'labels' have shifted over the years, although as a rule of thumb if you walk into a pub on a Saturday afternoon and it's full of men in Stone Island jackets, possibly sporting a single tiny metal badge with a crest on it, don't order the Babycham. In some respects, hooligans are the very definition of occult (which literally means 'hidden knowledge') with their initiations, codes and nose tapping rituals. Hooligan-speak, like that of any secret society, is full of ciphers, in-jokes and gestures that have become more obtuse as a response to police action, just as alternative religions feared persecution from the church in the past.

As yet, ducking and branding have not been introduced for football violence but there are those in the media and elsewhere who would see 'swimming' hooligans as an apt punishment.

Both football fans and occultists sometimes need to make a display of their power as a kind of invocation. Grand occasions in football are accompanied by a carnival riot of colour and exuberance normally associated with, well, carnivals or other bacchanalia. Things were not always so effervescent but, as the twentieth century progressed so flat caps became unfashionable as rattles and rosettes entered the stadia. Scarves in the team colours followed, to be joined by flags, banners, hats and, latterly, fright wigs, replica shirts, hair dye and face paint. The last of these skates amusingly close to the skin displays of the rituals of primitive tribesmen, while the full-scale fancy dress of some fans (particularly at end of season matches) taps right back into the symbolic costume wearing of English feast days and the more indiscriminate chaos of the lords of misrule.

Streamers and fireworks are frowned upon in the modern stadium, but old favourites like the flag forest and the scarf wall have been encouraged by clubs seeking to build atmosphere and sell more merchandise. For the fan, these displays are an exhibition of tribal power and unity, designed to intimidate the opposition and inspire their own side. The Latin American 'paper storm', where fragments of paper are hurled onto the pitch as the teams emerge, links straight into ancient practices associated with fertility rites and driving away evil spirits. It is unlikely that the brief vogue for toilet roll hurling at British games can claim the same pedigree, though this might conceivably have been a better comment on the game in progress, and was certainly related to the paper provided on the soccer special trains.

One modern drawback to displays of clannish might has been the sponsors' logo, since Hibs, Derby and Liverpool first introduced them. Initially, these were not worn for televised games so, to get around this, Coventry City wore a kit that incorporated the logo of the Talbot car into its design. Happily, this was another Coventry innovation that failed to go mainstream. However, it did address the key issue of how symbols work together; after all, the logo and colour comprise the club's brand identity, but the same is true for the identity of the kit manufacturer and sponsor. Some fans see the latter's intrusion as a desecration – one religion usurping another. If the allegations found on the wilder shores of the Internet are to be believed, this could be right in more ways than one; in a bid to come up with even more powerful images, some companies have apparently borrowed pagan and occult motifs.

Any supporter whose club sports the Umbro logo might be amused by the suggestion that it is based on the ancient native American symbol for the eye of the medicine man. Similarly, the Nike swoosh could be loosely approximated from the strongly occult ring of Saturn. Other adapted emblems include the red 'snake' in BT's logo and the 'yin and yang' of Pepsi Cola. Close examination of the Starbucks Coffee logo reveals a mermaid, and the Celtic Tree of Life can be discerned on Timberland boots. Therefore if British Telecom sponsors your team, and you are wearing Nike trainers and an Umbro shirt, you are actually sporting more pagan symbolism than the average Wiccan off to perform a ritual. And that's before taking the power of the club crest into consideration.

BT Symbol or snake?   **Pepsi cola or Yin and Yang?**   **Timberland or Celtic Tree of Life?**

Taken together, the badge, symbol, nickname and even mascot present the face of the team to the world. The club uses all of these in its marketing activities but, in occult terms, the fan is the most effective element when he uses them in various symbolic displays of power. These vary from the colour blocks presented by a multitude of fans wearing replica shirts or staging mass scarf displays, whether stretched for the singing of ballads or twirled during more vigourous demonstrations. The flag forest is more common in Europe than the UK, as are huge banners that stretch across whole ends. The point is to thrust one's colours and emblems into the face of the enemy, exactly as armies did in the past to intimidate and threaten their adversaries, as well as providing reassurance for one's own team. These are also the roles that amulets, symbols and talismans play in the occult: protection at one end, power at the other, and a belief in the symbol as a representation of the soul of the believer as a part of something greater than themselves. This being one of the things that supporting a team is all about.

1-0 to the Arsenal

Scoring one more and other important numbers

Mathematics is a language can't you read? This is perhaps how a fusion of Stephen Hawkings and Steven Morrissey might have put it. Former Scotland coach Craig Brown was more cryptic when he said 'they had a dozen corners, maybe twelve- I'm guessing.' Precision in numbers is important though because everything is a number, even the name of God, and if you get your numbers right then you have the key to the universe, a win on the lottery or a lucrative cup fixture away to one of the giants of the game.

Football, if it has nothing else, has important numbers in absolute abundance. Not just points for a win, goals scored or conceded but crowd figures, time added on, player salaries, numbers on shirts and of cups won. Then there are anniversaries, date of club's founding and that's before starting on the eighteen and six yard boxes or ones relating to size of pitch and length of minutes since scoring. Some formulate betting patterns and try to predict future outcomes by adding together a series of, seemingly unrelated, figures or soothsay around the number of substitutions over a given season. A pleasingly odd but nice sequence along these lines is that the ninth captain to win European Cup (Bobby Charlton) wore number nine, the tenth (Rivera) number ten and the fourteenth (Cruyff) number fourteen.

Then again Johann Cruyff was only number fourteen because when he started at Ajax someone else had the number nine. He became so attached to the number though that he refused to accept the sensible 1974 Dutch world cup squad listing of one upwards on an alphabetical basis under which he would be number one. Once started though the number madness spreads so Thierry Henry opted for number fourteen in honour of Cruyff. Some take this to an even more obtuse level as Liam Miller did at Celtic after being denied the number seven shirt which he wanted as an homage to Eric Cantona, he opted for forty three as this adds up to seven.

Supporters and players are full of number superstitions and try to manipulate patterns and see meaning where quite frankly there is none. In 1994 on April the twenty ninth Brazilian side Botofogo lost seven nil to Vasco da Gama. Seven years later the same day produced the same scoreline and in both matches the final goal was netted by da Gama's number seven. This confluence of sevens (nine minus two is also seven) brought massive soul searching amongst the Botofogo squad, officials and fans because seven is the number of God.

This is the essence of numerology, which refers to systems, traditions or beliefs in a mystical or esoteric relationship between numbers and physical objects or living things. Such 'numerological divination' was popular among early mathematicians as was a numerical explanation of the world, and ability to prophesise through figures. The term can also be used for those who, in the view of some observers, place excessive faith in numerical patterns, such as sports fans or investors, even if those people don't practice traditional numerology.

Modern numerology appears to be a fusion of teachings from Ancient Babylonia, Pythagoras in the sixth century BC, astrological philosophy from Hellenistic Alexandria, early Christian mysticism and the occultism of the Gnostics as well as the Hebrew Cabbalah. However no 'holistic' belief system would be complete without a dash of spice from far eastern sources tossed in and stirred well, even if as will become apparent later these traditions contradict each other. It is at once the most apparently scientific of the occult belief systems and yet the least predictable because of the sheer volume of possible outcomes. This means that parapsychologists, astrologers, theologians and others, football fans say, who seek anomalies to guide them to wisdom and an insight into the true nature of the universe can almost 'prove' whatever they like. To the occult statistician there is no such thing as a spurious correlation or as the famous number fourteen (Johann Cruyff) mentioned above put it 'coincidence is logical.'

Then again as psychologist John Ruscio notes; 'if you look in a fantastic number of places, and count anything that you stumble upon as supportive evidence, you are guaranteed to discover meaning where none exists.' Those who restack league tables by giving two points instead of three for a win for example are employing sound mathematical principles in much the same way that philosophy was used by theology during medieval times, selectively to prove only the points one wishes to. Football fans do this all the time and are like a drunk man using a lamppost for support, quoting numbers and statistics to bolster a position, rather than to offer illumination. Thus Everton fans will tell you, often in a tone of quiet desperation, that The Toffees are the most successful side in English football. This is true if the only criterion used is cumulative points in the top flight of English Football. Those involved in football, like numerologists everywhere, are adept at seeing the meaning they want by arranging the figures in a certain way. To quote Howard Wilkinson, 'if they hadn't scored, we would've won.'

There are so many numerical combinations that it's easy, often using the same basic statistics, to 'prove' completely opposite patterns. So for example the comment that: 'it's been fifty years since Reading came back from one nil to Scottish opposition' might indicate that something is either unlikely or long overdue. In actual fact of course Reading so rarely play Scottish clubs competitively that like many footballing 'facts' it is so obscure as to be irrelevant. Often when a real pattern emerges it is regarded almost with supernatural awe such as Cardiff City beating Leeds United two one three years running at the same stage of the FA Cup in the nineteen fifties.

The attractiveness of numerology to the average supporter comes from the desire to find somebody who will tell you that your team are full of hidden strengths and powers. At times, each of us is vulnerable. We feel unloved, misunderstood, confused, or rudderless, we need comforting statistics to cling to after our team has been prison sexed by some superior outfit. Numbers soothe and managers know this so they say things like; 'our keeper only had one save to make but we lost 4-0' (Craig Brown again) or 'we must have had 99% of the game. It was the other three per cent that cost us the match' (Ruud Gullit). Perhaps top is Gerard Houllier's flexible definition of being number one: 'You can't say my team aren't winners. They've proved that by finishing fourth, third and second in the last three years.'

Houllier's confused approach to arithmetic aside, numbers, to a numerologist, actually have a resonance that goes well beyond luck or patterns relevant in a given situation such as a scoreline. Every number from zero to ten relates to an aspect of life and has its own meaning. To give a few examples; one stands for individuality and aggression, two is balance and seven is thought. This numerical linking to meaning is simplified by being reduced down to a single digit via a process known as Digit Summing. Taking Colchester United's average home crowd of 5508 for 2007-2008 the following 'meaning' can be abstracted. $5+5 + 0+8 (0+8) = 8$. Eight is the number of thought and consciousness, which considering the mighty U's season might be best avoided. Three highlights issues of communication and interaction as well as neutrality and the number nine completion. Four is creation, five action, seven responsibility and ten rebirth. This also works with words as values correspond to each letter's position in the alphabet from a being one to z being twenty six. This can of course result in team name's having a meaning but unless you have a long train journey ahead, to Inverness say, you might want to take it on trust that Inverness Caledonian Thistle are zero if you digit sum them down. This is a number of great transformation or change, which is clearly true in terms of relegation if that is the number of points collected.

It is one thing to use numbers to analyse or interpret but is it possible to use them to predict the future as Paul Simpson suggested in this pile up of World Cup statistics about the 2002 final that all pointed in one direction.

> Winners: Argentina: $1978 + 1986 = 3964$
> Winners: Germany: $1974 + 1990 = 3964$
> Winners: Brazil: $1970 + 1994 = 3964$
> Winners: Brazil: $1962 + ???? = 3964$

The number that should be where the question marks are is of course 2002 when Brazil beat Germany 2-0.

Football fans are adept at all kinds of number crunching involving playing records, average gates, and goals scored at times of games. All these can offer meaning and hope where there is apparently none. Chanting a mantra of great feats offers comfort as when Koppites sing 'we won it five times' about the European Cup to compensate for another failed tilt at the English league title or Evertonians reminding people that they've won that league title nine times. Which is the most you can win anything by according to Bobby Robson who, clearly underestimating the scale that mathematics operates on, once said 'we got nine and you can't score more than that.'

There is a period in every fans' life when they are able to reel off not only the statistics for their own team but also results from across the division. Today computers have scattered this up to the stratosphere with the ability to compile and easily compare fabulous oceans of trivia. The media aids in this occasionally showing league tables according to what would have happened if the games had stopped after sixty six minutes and only English born players' goals counted. But just because one can collate statistics doesn't mean one should because it usually means someone will find a use for them eventually. This is quite possibly how the European Fair Play League came about with its immediate Europa League spot and complex system of judging fair play.

Still at least UEFA had a sort of rationale. There are other areas of football where numbers are far more random. The numbered shirt was first adopted in the 1933 FA Cup final between Everton (who had one to eleven) and Manchester City (twelve to twenty two) and it was not mandatory in the Football League until 1939 (1946 in Scotland). Although in some leagues shirt numbers are still strictly on a one to eleven basis for players on the pitch, in many the correspondence of player to position and shirt number is increasingly strained. This is made even more complex when teams withdraw shirts as is common in Italy where the most popular 'retired' number is ten. Three (Maldini) and six (Baresi) are drawing their pension, and made sacred, by AC Milan and can only be worn by those players' sons. Long or exemplary service to club or nation are the most common reason to remove a number but sometimes it is to mark a tragedy. Marc Vivien Foe actually had two numbers withdrawn (seventeen for Lyon and twenty three for Lens) after his untimely death in 2003.

David Beckham has never expressed an interest in the writer William Burroughs nor the scientist John Nash yet both would have been very interested in his choice of twenty three as his shirt number. They are not alone as the number is sacred to believers in chaos magic and it runs through history from the 23rd psalm onwards linking Charles Darwin, the bombing of Hiroshima (bomb was dropped at 8.15am - 8+15= 23), William Shakespeare and Julius Caesar. All human life is based on the number with each parent contributing 23 chromosomes and in Chinese numerology it symbolises marriage, procreation, and progeny.

The number also interests mathematicians because it is made up of two consecutive prime numbers, including the only even one, whilst being a prime in itself.

Beckham says he selected 23 in deference to "magic" Michael Jordan the basketball player and is probably unaware about the mythology around the number or the fact that he has added to it. He may be unimpressed that the first the first Morse code transmission message (what hath God wrought) is from the Numbers verse 23 line 23 but "23 skidoo" (to make a swift exit) is something he's definitely familiar with. He should also perhaps also be aware of its association with disaster in films and real life. This returns us to William Burroughs who met the captain (called Clark) of a ferry between Spain and Morocco. Just prior to the ferry sinking Clark informed the writer that he had been doing the route for 23 years without incident. Burroughs was musing on this event when a radio news report announced the crash of a Flight 23 on the New York-Miami route piloted by another Captain Clark. Worth mentioning as well is that the player who broke David Beckham's metatarsal and caused all that heartache a few years ago (Aldo Duscher) was wearing number twenty three at the time.

Players can set great store by their numbers even if, as noted earlier, they initially come by them accidentally such as Ivan Zamorano who was given eighteen (1+8) at Inter Milan because Ronaldo was number nine. Sometimes there is a logic behind the choice, a player's birthday or honouring a hero but some might consider that Ballack is tempting fate by wearing thirteen even if it is a tribute to Rudi Voller. A star's insistence on a certain number is now an additional complication to transfer negotiations which previously might have revolved around prestige of say being the recognised number nine at a side.

There are also those who wish to avoid certain numbers which is why Kaka ended up at number eight. Eight is a key number in the Wiccan belief system, it is also considered highly lucky by the Chinese. This is because the word for eight sounds similar to the one for wealth and in some dialects fortune. The Beijing Olympics began on August the eighth in 2008 at eight seconds past eight minutes on the eighth hour. Number plates and telephone number featuring multiple eights fetch a high value on the open market. There is also a resemblance between 88 and the phrase double joy as well as the eight spokes in the Buddhist wheels and eight beatitudes in the Sermon on the Mount.

So number eight would seem like a good choice for an aspirant

World superstar. That is except in Belgium (and some other countries) where 88 and 18 are linked to the far right (88 being HH or Heil Hitler and 18 being AH or Adolf Hitler). Kaka's actual reasons were much more practical as he didn't want the number five shirt offered because that was associated with the great Zinedine Zidane. Rather than compete, Kaka decided to be the legendary number eight rather than a replacement number five. Three clubs have retired a number eight (most notably Dynamo Ceske Budejovice for Karel Poborksy) and Hristo Stoitchkov was mighty for Bulgaria in the 1994 World Cup but in the world of modern football these could not touch Kaka, except maybe Zinedine.

Just as players have their preferred numbers so certain teams believe in the power of a particular number combined with the shirt. This gives rise to the veneration of the number seven at Manchester United, nine at Newcastle and elsewhere or number ten for Brazil. These links are usually based on a particular great player or run of great players in a position over the years. This becomes ingrained in the culture of the club causing fans to wistfully yearn for a great lumbering T Rex of a centre forward when actually what's required is a nippy velociraptor in the midfield. So perhaps the Italians and others who remove the shirts are actually being quite canny in enabling the fans to remember the greats of the past without letting in any misty eyed infringement on future buying policy. It also allows fans a 'safe' name and number on their shirt, someone who will stay and not be lured away by a dream move to Hadjik Split after half a season.

Several clubs leave a number blank for their fans. In many cases, from Aberdeen to Zenit St. Petersburg via Bristol Rovers, Grimsby Town and others, it is the number twelve. This presumably relates to concept of the crowd as the twelfth man roaring the team on and the notion of spectator influencing events has a good history right back to the Coliseum crowds intervening to save a gladiator's life. Quite why Reading and Norwich reserve the number thirteen is harder to assess, though possibly it is the notion that thirteen is unlucky, after that incident with the last supper, therefore it is better not to have it on the pitch. Panathinaikos have a more solid reason for using that number which is to honour their Ultras who enter the ground at Gate Thirteen. Other numbers allocated to the faithful include thirty one at Bristol City and forty at Oldham Athletic.

Another magic realm is the score, not just in the sense of getting more goals than the opposition but the glory of a 5-0 drubbing or a hard fought 3-2 or, for Arsenal fans of a certain age, a solid 1-0 pile driver. So happy did this score line make them that they had a cheerful chant that simply ran one nil to the Arsenal. This was not in the expectation of more goals but in the delighted satisfaction, backed up by statistics that once they reached that position the result was assured. The chant was an attempt to hypnotise the opposition into accepting the result as inevitable. On a side note there is a team in the Russian lower leagues actually called Arsenal Two which must be confusing for people reading out the score.

Alongside magic scorelines there are also golden years for teams, whether club or national. In England of course it is 1966 because that was, as the advertising slogan ran, when Eric Cantona was born. 1966 holds a hex over English football like no other, it is a dream and curse, the bringer of the thirty (now over forty) years of hurt referred to in the 1996 song Three Lions. These are many in the game who cling on in the belief that history may repeat itself in the following decade. Spurs fans set great store by there being a one in the year because they won the league in 1951 and 1961, the FA Cup (1991, 1981, 1961,1921, 1901) and the League Cup (1971). Those with a longer term view, hope for repetition in the subsequent century. A likely upshot of the latter may be that in fifteen years or so there could be a whole lot of unwarranted excitement in Huddersfield as the centenary of their greatest side approaches. Then again there is no reason why history should not repeat as even the mightiest have their lean years and professional football in England has been cyclical over its first full century. To take an example Eric Cantona was a year old when Manchester United won the league in 1967 but he would wait until he was twenty five and playing for them before they won it again in 1992 and this gap included relegation to the second tier of English football.

This is not just an English disease. After a series of disasters associated with the number seventeen a Scottish newspaper was able to report with glee that the Caledonians were playing Italy on that date which has ancient and modern bad luck associations for Italians.

The Roman numeral for seventeen (XVII) can be rearranged to VIXI the past tense of lived (i.e. to be dead) and some venues have no row or rooms seventeen. In footballing terms Italy have played eleven and won four of the games on that date over the past 30 years including the 17th of July defeat to Brazil on penalties in the 1994 World Cup final. Their twelfth game (the one against Scotland) went to form rather than misfortune with Italy winning away 2-1.

This highlights a very localised faith in an unlucky number but some cultures have totally different schemata when it comes to numbers and fortune. Number two is considered fortunate in many Asian cultures as good things come in pairs so often positive symbols are doubled up. Three is associated with birth and hence new beginnings whilst four is avoided at all costs as in some far Eastern languages it sounds similar to the word for death. Some buildings have no "fourth" floor and teams are reluctant to trot out in a four four two (death death doubled) formation. The number fourteen is similarly afflicted but five is a positive stable number associated with leadership and six considered right for business whilst seven is good for rising up so a top one for sides with promotion hopes. Eight is mentioned elsewhere and nine has associations with royalty. Alternatively in the wrong combinations six may mean decline but six hundred and sixty six (an unlikely squad number even at Manchester City) is a positive number in the East but the number of the beast in the west.

It is easy to see that with all those possible significant dates and numbers how numerology might be a perfect fit with football fans but less so how it might actually affect the outcome of a match. Unless you are Uri Geller who lifted a curse on Newcastle United that meant they could actually win a game in London. Uri explained that;

> 'It is about positive thinking. Even if you are not there but hundreds or even thousands of miles away, it would all connect with a spiritual thought through which we can transmit energy. This is a lot do with the number eleven. Newcastle had not won in twenty nine games in London and two and nine is eleven. Number eleven is a mystical, powerful number, it is an awakening call, also an alert.'

A Newcastle paper, *The Chronicle*, called on Uri Geller after earlier attempts by fans, which included exorcists and witch doctors and even flying two stuffed magpies to London miles in a private jet failed, though why flying stuffed magpies anywhere should have any effect is open to conjecture. Geller asked readers of the Chronicle to channel their belief in winning through pictures of him in the paper. When the result came in the following day a triumphant *Chronicle* trumpeted the headline Arsenal 1, Spoon Army 3. Arsene Wenger was quoted as saying it 'was like there was a sorcerer at work' as the Magpies flew to the top of the premiership with their first win in London against any team for four years. There were strange scenes at the match with two sending offs, a penalty and the normally calm Thierry Henry lost his temper with the referee. Henry had scored first and Arsenal bossed the first half but Uri had an explanation for this. He claims he was late and ticketless but the moment he touched Highbury Ray Parlour was sent off. Then after predicting a Shearer penalty he ran round the outside of the ground eleven times to lift the hoodoo. Perhaps foolishly the staff at Arsenal had let him in.

It is one thing to recognize that much in the universe can be explained by reduction to mathematical formulae, and that formulae can be tested and demonstrated to be accurate or not. It is quite another to claim that somehow a random series of numbers and letters can tell the future. Galileo's assertion that nature is written in the language of mathematics should not really be applied to the number of times a given player has come on as a substitute against lower opposition and scored. This does not stop football fans praying at the house of numbers. Most especially it doesn't prevent the more desperate to boldly enter the field of quantum physics and try to stop time, speed it up, or in some cases make it go backwards to alter a result or give their team a better chance. This is allied to the creative mathematics of the relegation threatened side or the desperate attempt to make the figures fit better and give grounds for hope. Or as former manager of Shrewsbury Town Ian McNeil put it, 'we got the winner with three minutes left, but then they equalised.'

Sir Alex Ferguson is famous for his watch gesturing actions to referees and when he takes his team abroad insists on keeping to British time throughout the period away, at least in Europe. More ambitiously Bill Shankly kept to UK time whilst on a pre season tour of America and these time lords have a point. It is part of keeping things regular and controlling the situation which is part of their job, even if according to recent studies managers overall only effect five percent of the outcome of games.

One other source of fresh hope comes with the injection of new personnel through the transfer market. There is the magic of transfer fees where according to the interests of the clubs involved, and in some cases the media, the same deal can be presented as a fifteen million pound transfer, ten million pound transaction or somewhere in between in the case of Jermaine Defoe's move to Tottenham depending on how the sell on clauses are weighed up. The usual rule is that the selling club Couches up the figure and the buying one Bartons it down but there are exceptions to this such as when a club wishes to make a point of how much money it has to spend. This 'peacock financing' attracts agents' interests and makes the club seem a good bet for ambitious players even if that is not always the way things work out as the careers of Scott Parker and Sean Wright-Phillips show. Both of those followed the money rather than a first team place and lost their international careers as a result. The converse is the irony that the richer successful clubs often can bid less than other teams because players prefer to play for them over a less flourishing rival.

This is the Lescott in the room when it comes to football and numbers in recent years because with notable and amusing exceptions (Newcastle United) the teams that pay the highest salaries win the most because they are able to offer the players what they want financially. There are individual exceptions to this player wise (a couple are mentioned above) but a swift glance at the league tables over the past decade shows that in general the teams with the biggest wage bills come top. This does not hold lower down the league nor is it entirely new as the history of football is littered with big spending successful sides but the correlation is much closer now with players' freer than ever to negotiate higher salaries. Part of the dark magic of football is also that several of these same successful high wage clubs also have the greatest levels of debt in the game that under anything approaching a normal business model would be unsustainable.

At the heart of all this number crunching is the manager who has to get the digits right on the pitch and also, in most clubs, keep a reasonably balanced sheet off it. These are the crucial numbers of management and if they are not reached then the result is dismissal. In 2002 Chris Hope at the Judge Institute of Management came up with a mathematical formula to decide when it is wise to sack a coach. Match results were weighted and analysed and two key externals considered. These are the length of honeymoon period for a new manager and how much importance to put on the most recent games. Expectations of fans, money spent on transfers and morale boosting cup runs were not considered. The key factor though is what they describe as the 'trapdoor', this is the points per game average which they found should be at least 0.74. Their optimum honeymoon period is eight weeks and 47% weighting should be given to the last five games. Relegation threatened clubs adopting this formula would increase the points accumulated over a season by five.

So it should all be simple shouldn't it? Football however does not go in for simplicity and science when there are so many other factors involved and over the time studied managers (John Gregory and Walter Smith to name two) were kept on whilst others (Joe Royle, Gianluca Vialli and Ruud Gullit) were fired completely against the sense of the formula, but very much in line with the irrational nature of football. This is also in keeping with the average fan who, whilst unable to change actual results, is quite happy manipulating figures to better suit their own perception of reality.

It is not just fans who do this, in fact many people who would regard themselves as real supporters oppose what they see as a Premier League and Sky Sports driven attempt to redraw the history of football. This recent re-evaluation treats the top division so it starts in 1992, rather than nearer 1892, as if the current league is somehow an entirely different entity from what went before. Certainly many magic numbers are involved for teams reaching the English Premiership that seem to defy all sense of economics or relationship to the division immediately below. A couple of years ago the average Premier League side received forty five times the television income of one in the Championship. Within the league itself the amount of money required to buy success has moved from multi millions (Jack Walker and Blackburn Rovers) to hundreds (Roman Abramovich and Chelsea) and beyond. Money has always mattered in the game though with Preston North End's nineteenth century 'invincibles' bankrolled by illegal payments to players and embezzlement by Major William Sudell, the secretary cum manager of PNE. Sudell not only flouted the FA ruling that players should be born six miles from a ground or have lived in an area for two years he also bought success by stealing a small fortune from the cotton mill he also managed. That small fortune was £5,326, less than a third of the weekly wage of even an average Premier League player today and 100,000 times less than the debt Manchester United run in 2010. Sudell always meant to pay back his employers and never benefited financially himself but got a three year sentence when the numbers failed to add up.

For most us who follow the game the results of our miscalculations are not so great. However we may all recognise the truth in what St. Augustine of Hippo, who lived in the fourth century, when he wrote 'numbers are the Universal language offered by the deity to humans as confirmation of the truth.' Similar to Pythagoras, St. Augustine believed that everything had numerical relationships and it was up to the mind to seek and investigate the secrets of these relationships or have them revealed by divine grace and there was of course the Holy Trinity in football (Alan Ball, Brian Labone and Howard Kendall). All such search for meaning and divinity and truth comes as scant recompense on a rainy day in Stoke as an away fan trudging from Britannia Stadium reflects that the universal language and truth has left one's side a goal down and that the instrument of 'divine grace' was James Beattie.

Abide with me

Songs, chants and invocations

Whether collectively or alone, singing in praise of one's God, chanting prayers in call and response, and rhythmic drumming or clapping to achieve an altered state are all features of religious ceremonies and, of course, of the football stadium. The purpose is to heighten emotions, achieve a desired end and to express collective faith through ritualised tribal songs that draw attention to one's fanaticism and to declare allegiance to a cause. This may or may not coincide with other activities, such as the use of instruments, candles, incense or indeed fire, and it is not uncommon for each activity to end in communion or sacrifice. It's just that, in football, the dropping of a player or sacking of a manager is rarely fatal and the alcohol drunk at communion is unlikely to be altar wine.

The rise in collective singing at matches mirrors the decline in church attendance since the 1950s. This might have suggested that people really just like a bit of a singsong and it was only the venue that had changed, except that football gates also dwindled gradually from the 1950s, hitting a low in the late 1980s. Both were affected by alternative leisure pursuits, greater mobility, the fracturing of communities and, in the case of football, the rise in hooliganism. Three disasters in quick succession at Heysel, Bradford and Hillsborough in the mid- to late-1980s that resulted in the death of many fans provoked a crisis in English football. On a happier note, the growth of acid house and popularity of the drug ecstasy gave rise to the second summer of love in 1988 when, whilst Manchester United fans screamed 'accciieeddd!!' at their bemused Wimbledon hosts, 'massive' clubs like Spurs and Newcastle were recording gates of just over 10,000 (about the same size as the larger raves). Football attendances have since picked up, from a low of 16.5 million a season to double that today. This puts crowds back to late-1950s levels, but they remain well short of their 1949 peak of 41 million. Church attendances also seem to have levelled out since the 1990s, while figures for alternative or minority religions continue to increase.

As yet, other faiths haven't supplied the terraces with many anthems, easy though it would be to adapt the Hare Krishna chant to anyone called Harry. Instead, supporters base their songs on secular tunes, whether folk or popular, or ones from the established church. Whole songs have been stolen from the Christian church, such as When the Saints Go Marching In, or tunes like Lord of the Dance and once starting a match with a hymn was not restricted to the cup final. This borrowing of religious songs, rituals and even in some cases forms of worship might be sacrilegious or even devilish to some, but the real tribal and cultish element is subtler than that and lies in the belief that words can change events. One aspect is that the collective force of the crowd will transmit itself to the players via the noise they make and another that it can summon or channel the spirits of the past to help in the present.

In the 1960s, an early episode of the BBC's Panorama examined the Kop at Anfield with the same kind of anthropological treatment one might use to study a primitive tribe. In particular, it was the swaying, singing and displays of totems, reminiscent of voodoo ceremonies, which interested the film makers. Voodoo, drumming, chanting and swaying helps shift people into an alternative state of consciousness; in football, the hope is that the chants, in themselves, can help transport the fans and team to a different plane, whether positive (for one's own side) or negative (for the opposition). A more likely outcome is that fans can act to magnify what's already occurring, so a team that is playing well may play better with a vocal crowd behind them.

Norwich City, a side not normally associated with singing despite their songbird nickname and whatever Delia Smith may think, have the oldest club song of any team, with On the Ball, City going back a century. Newcastle United's Blaydon Races is equally venerable, though initially less club-specific. The songs themselves need not have sacred or local roots and can be borrowed from anywhere: musicals, traditional airs, music hall (which we have to thank for the various renditions of My Old Man) as well as popular hits. In a strange process, opposite to that of the hymn as football song, some secular ditties have become near religious for the devotees of particular clubs. Examples include Blowing Bubbles at West Ham or Glad All Over at Crystal Palace. Lyrics are not essential; Everton fans 'sing' the theme to 1960s cop show Z-Cars (based on the folk tune Johnny Todd) at away matches in an attempt magically to make the game a home one.

Usually, it is the simplest, sweetest songs that have proved most popular at football stadia. These include reinterpretations of Boney M's Holiday, the Ronettes' Winter Wonderland and Middle of the Road's Chirpy Chirpy Cheep Cheep. Go West by the Pet Shop Boys is another favourite. This has as much to do with the ability of thousands of tone deaf, excitable people spread out over hundreds of yards to carry a complex tune, as how far a given song has permeated local or national consciousness. More complex songs are rarely heard though Manchester City's reworking of Oasis' Wonderwall and Manchester United's adaptation of the classic Joy Division song Love will Tear us Apart, which become Giggs will Tear you Apart, Again are good examples. The fact that both records are by Manchester bands, with that added element of local passion, has almost certainly helped.

Over the course of a game, the chants may move from optimistic to mournful, often via gloating, hopeful and threatening. However much the mood may alter with the game, one study has shown that, perhaps surprisingly, less than half of the songs have any direct relation to activities on the pitch. The study used a very small but thorough sample at Oxford United home games in the 1970s. It tested for event-timed chants (like How High do you Want the Goal? when an opposing team shot over) and unrelated ditties such as Oxford Boys We are Here. The latter made up over 60% of the chants and occurred at regular intervals. This was borne out by a less detailed study involving four other clubs during the same period. Collected anecdotal evidence from a number of grounds later in the twentieth century and into the twenty-first bears this out too. Newcastle fans in the 1990s, for example, didn't actually need to be playing Sunderland to inform anyone listening that Peter Reid Eats Bananas with his Feet and Spurs' presence was not required for Arsenal fans to shout various complimentary verses about them. Songs do respond to refereeing decisions, goals, diving cheats or sending-offs, but the many are non-specific beyond, obviously, the support of the team or denigration of a rival, whether or not they are playing that team on any particular day. This is normal in any faith; think of the consistently hard time the devil is given in churches where he is unlikely to be present.

Football chants can be divided into subsections such as invocations, initiations, consecrations, incantations and desecrations, as well as event-specific rituals, and can be to do with protection, worship, statement of faith and threat. Within these categories, songs might be bitter or joyous, celebratory or ironic. Wiccan chanting can be divided along very similar lines and for exactly the same purposes, although they don't do threats or cursing (but there are occult traditions that do). Just to demonstrate how easy it is to cross over from spells to sport, below are a couple of chants. The second, admittedly lifted from the film The Craft, might do well to stoke up the atmosphere at a big game whilst, with minor alterations, the first might suit a relegated side from an agricultural area.

> 'Hoof and horn, hoof and horn
> All that dies shall be reborn
> Corn and grain, corn and grain
> All that falls shall rise again.'

> 'Now is the time,
> now is the hour,
> I am the magick,
> I am the power.'

To a first time match attendee, all songs are in a sense an initiation to a fraternity and with each fresh one learned and sung, the more snugly one fits into the congregation. Occult initiations are more individual, studied and dramatic but serve the same function of welcoming a new member into the mysteries. They also tend to take a very long time and rely on the newcomer learning through observation. As one initiate joked, 'Your first year as a voodoo trainee involves plucking chickens and your second year is still plucking chickens but a bit closer to the ceremony'. Not so dissimilar to several management training schemes, and certainly close to match day learning, which relies heavily on newcomers picking up the rituals for themselves. Watch any youngster at a game for the first time, particularly an away fixture, and it's possible to see them mentally filing away codes of behaviour so they know when to ironically applaud abusive chants and when to shout back.

There is a very useful term used by witches: 'raising the power'. It basically means getting everyone in the mood for the activities that follow. It performs the same function as the vigorous pre-match chanting at football. In football, the fans arriving at a ground and singing there do this afresh with every visit. Very often, there is an order of service for home games, climaxing just prior to kick off with the main club hymn. The order may alter if there are immediate pressing issues, such as a protest against the board, but the pre-kick-off song is sacrosanct. The agenda for away fans is different and will usually start off with a clear statement of identity, followed by abuse of their nearest rivals (to show who they are not) before rounding on their hosts' failings, whether historical or current, relating to players or their ground. Prior to kick-off, the away support will revert to a simple statement of identity and attempt to drown out the home team's anthem. So that's how it works in football. In Wicca, as mentioned in the chapter on Clothes and colours, Wiccans consecrate an area by placing candles at the four points of the compass, which is why an actual compass is an essential part of the Wiccan wardrobe. They complete this process with the following chant:

> 'Guardians of the East be present with us
> Guardians of the South be present with us
> Guardians of the West be present with us
> Guardians of the North be present with us.'

Wiccans don't have to alter their order of service, as they are always the home team, but this chant doubles up as both a consecration and an invocation. This sort of blessing or seeking of helpful energy should not be confused with the evocation of spirits which is more akin to sorcery (the raising of servitor or servant spirit). In football, invocations are often straightforward pleas for a team to do something specific or just generally improve, like the groaning 'All we are saying is give us a goal' (to the tune of Give Peace a Chance) or repetitive chants like 'Come on you Clarets, come on you Clarets'. There is often a slightly exasperated tone to these, an attempt to drag the team forward by sheer will and belief. Some of the more complex ones overlap with the songs to do with identity and faith whereby the invocation calls upon the tribal elders or past heroes as a means of steadying the nerves of the current squad. An excellent example of this is The Fields of Anfield Road, based on a faux-Irish folk song, The Fields of Athenry about an

Irish prisoner who'll never see his sweetheart again. In the Liverpool version, it anchors the spectators of today to the glorious past of Bill Shankly and Bob Paisley. The chorus runs:

> 'All round the fields of Anfield Road,
> Where once we watched the king Kenny play, (and could he play!)
> We had Heighway on the wing,
> We had dreams and songs to sing,
> Of the glory round the fields of Anfield Road.'

In an occult context, the above invocation might be the summoning of a force, sending helpful energy or channelling a spirit into the practitioner. The devotee is imploring the intervention of a being to drive forward a successful venture, in a clear case of ancestor worship. Many clubs have similar means of telling players what they should aspire to and to hopefully imbue the present squad with some of the attributes of previous giants. Sometimes fans deliberately sing songs from another era because they are bored or wish to remind the current team whose boots they are filling.

Such 'encouragement' can easily slip over into protective songs which essentially support the team by casting a defensive spell and, whilst they do express tribalism, are defiant and loving in the way they work. They are a collective demonstration of identity designed to reassure the faithful about who they are and instill the team with a sense of belief. Most club anthems would come into this category, from Glory Glory Tottenham Hotspur through to the various laments like Blue Moon or 'chin up' songs such as Birmingham City's Keep Right on to the End of the Road. The list is pretty much endless – some funny, some sad, none more so than Nottingham Forest's version of Mull of Kintyre. *

Forest are a truly unique team in British football, and not just because they pioneered the use of shin pads. After a relatively modest century of existence in which they won two FA Cups and few promotions, they went into overdrive between 1977 and 1980. In that short time, they won the League Cup twice, the Football League and two European cups, making them the second most successful British team in that competition. For the next decade, they remained an attractive First Division side, with good runs in the cup including reaching the final in

---

* Actually there possibly is one chant sadder and this comes from the supporters of the Bolivian national side, which loosely translated runs Long live Bolivia with its beautiful coastline. This is only remarkable when one learns that Bolivia lost its entire coastline in an ill-fated war against Chile in 1883.

1991. Shortly after this, they were relegated and have hardly troubled the top flight of English football since. The words are most appropriate to remind themselves and others just how great they were:

'How far we have travelled and what places we've seen,
Goodison and Anfield are places we've been,
Maine Road and Old Trafford have rung to the sound,
of the boys from the Trent and the old City Ground.'

Forest fans are linking themselves by association to some top teams in English football, which they themselves still were when the song was first sung. The function is to weave a cocoon around the team and fans to make them stand firm, even in defeat, and to console during times of trouble. The magic is the warm feeling of belonging, a special status that engenders the hope that maybe those days will return. It echoes the story of Arthur Pendragon, the once and future king, who will rise again when the situation demands it. The chances of the magical Brian Clough returning are, of course, small, and even their song is now dated – before too long, neither Goodison nor Anfield may exist and Maine Road has already disappeared.

Sometimes the statement of identity or faith needs to be stronger and more defiant, less protective lullaby and more assertive proclamation, although this doesn't stop some of them being used as lullabies by certain parents. Anxiety, anger or trouble bring out a more aggressive identity or defiant avowal, however. Sometimes designed to intimidate, they are always vociferous. Again, there are more of these than there are teams in the League, but surely nothing sums up slightly self-pitying, violent pride and defiance than the use to which Millwall supporters have put Rod Stewart's Sailing. Their version has everything a necromancer's prayer requires, such as honesty, clear intention and purpose. There is also a willingness to welcome in and cherish a negative image (or at least, an image that others see as negative), and never let it go. It runs:

'You don't like us. You don't like us. No one likes us. We don't care.
We are Millwall. We are Millwall. Super Millwall. From the Den.'

Another team with traditionally frisky fans are Leeds United, whose relegation from the top division this century prompted an incredible display of rage and impassioned belonging, rather than the usual mopey-looking scarf-wearer weeping or defiantly clapping. Towards the end of the last game of the season against Arsenal, the Londoners decided to goad their Yorkshire visitors with the (ultimately unlikely) observation that they'd 'never play them again'. This provoked the Leeds following into a screaming, impassioned, deafening chorus that went on and on and on, of: 'We are Leeds! We are Leeds! We are Leeds!' Shirts off, fists up, spittle flying, men, women and children turned into an army of dispossessed rage. At that moment they were truly legion, abandoning self and merging into a collective monster of raging fury. If you ever want to know what it's like to achieve loss of individuality and become briefly a creature of united instinct and will, which is after all what many bacchanalian rituals promise, then a ticket to the relegation of a team with bonkers supporters should do the trick. It would certainly be cheaper and less time-consuming than learning a complex spell, and would definitely require less preparation.

At the less extreme end of the identity spectrum can be found Chelsea's reinterpretation of Lord of the Dance ('Carefree, wherever we may be, we are the famous CFC'), the many versions of Guantanamera, and Wrexham's interesting reworking of Anarchy in the UK ('I am a Wrexhamian, I am a North Walian...'). The point about all of these is that they separate the singers from the rest, imbuing the faithful with a special status that sets them apart. Whilst any Wiccan might be appalled at the setting oneself above humanity and nature, those interested in darker matters of power and domination would recognise these songs for what they are: a call to greater faith, to strengthen the collective identity against the outsider, to combine against the common foe and hopefully, just like any binding spell, to prevent an opponent acting normally.

In particular, there is a desire to stop an opponent's hero playing normally whilst urging one's own on through worship. Sometimes this takes the physical form of bowing down before the hero but more often it is in the form of a song of praise. The emotions engendered by the talismanic player might not be quite the same as those felt by a medieval peasant when a saint came to the local village but there is a crossover into the realms of faith in the desire to praise and thank and bless the hero. The worship a team or specific player is perhaps unsurprising, given that so many clubs owe their formation to the church, and this makes the tendency to adapt church hymns almost fitting. Although what the good fathers of St. Domingo's would have made of 'One goal at a time, Bob Latchford' is anyone's guess. Then again, they might have taken an equally dim view of the liberal tosh it was based on ('One day at a time, sweet Jesus'). Latchford was a goal-scoring legend but sometimes the hero may be a relatively minor part of the team's pantheon. Ole Gunner Solskjaer was never the greatest player at Old Trafford in the 1990s but he was always there, and inspired a deep affection. This resulted in a rather touching version of You are my Sunshine, the last part runs 'Alan Shearer, he may be dearer, but don't take our Solskjaer away'.

It is a good sign for a player to have their own song – well, in most cases anyway –as it indicates a certain career progression in terms of the fans' affection or, if it is derogatory, from opposing fans. It is almost embarrassing to write this, but people need heroes and in context (i.e. on the pitch) footballers can provide this. I am unlikely ever to forget watching as a boy Duncan Mackenzie do things to the Nottingham Forest defence that, as an adult, I would describe as obscene or sublime or just plain well, magic. For some reason, 'We all agree Duncan Mackenzie is magic' was indicative of a series of chants using the M-word in the mid to late 1970s. Not that Duncan wasn't magic – he could smoke at half-time, jump over Minis and do all sorts of tricks.

Sometimes, however, fans come not to praise but to bury, curse or desecrate. These are not simple songs teasing opponents about the score or style of play, designed to unsettle and annoy opposing teams. Rather, these songs are designed to wound, incite, enrage and humiliate. As Desmond Morris says in *The Soccer Tribe*:

> 'Nothing is too vicious for the cheerful bands of chanters, from
> implications of sexual inadequacy or abnormality, to suggestions
> of lunacy and advanced alcoholism... personal problems or human
> weakness is ruthlessly exploited in song after song. If no such
> weaknesses exist, they are happily invented.'

Fortunately, the shrieking callousness of the British press and online rumour rooms provide an endless supply of material, ranging from the libellous to valid social comment, from the amusing to the truly horrible. Nor is the abuse directed only at the players themselves; their friends, family, wives or girlfriends, pretty much anyone is considered fair game as long as it winds up not only the team on the pitch but also the supporters off it. Top footballers routinely have the paternity of their children questioned to the theme from Dad's Army of all things, with the lyrics changed to 'Who do you think you are kidding highly paid superstar if you think the baby's yours'. On the other hand, Celtic fans' critique of Paul Gascoigne for hitting his wife Sheryl was both cruel and accurate ('if you cannae beat the Ajax beat your wife'), after Glasgow Rangers had been put out of the European Cup by the Dutch team.

Sometimes it is the actual supporters, whether collectively or individually, who are the butt of a song that is deliberately designed to stir up hatred, defile a memory or in any other way turn an atmosphere ugly. The point here is less about the game (although it could be argued that added spite can help one side over another) and more about certain fans expressing tribal venom. Into this category fit songs about the loss of life in the Munich air disaster and the death of ninety-six Liverpool fans at Hillsborough. Lesser, though still grave offences include the disruption of a minute's silence for a particular team's hero or references to events unrelated to football that have touched a particular community. Notts County supporter, and mass murdering doctor, Harold Shipman, would no doubt be surprised at his name being invoked (to the tune of a toffee advert) at games involving teams from greater Manchester. The response whipped up by such songs can often spill over into violence and is the equivalent of cursing someone horribly but, as Wiccans know, curses are dangerous and have the habit of rebounding on their instigator.

Another popular provocation is to skit a rival's favourite songs, chorusing, 'You'll never walk again' at Liverpool or 'I'm forever throwing bottles' at West Ham. These are part of a wider repertoire of threatening songs, which are football's war chants (although 'You're going home in a fucking ambulance' or the delightful 'You're going to get your fucking heads kicked in' are rarely heard today). They can be directed against the officials, opposing team or supporters and, in spirit anyway, some of them sound incredibly like calls for demonic possession or a celebration of evil forces. What could be more bacchanalian, more of an invocation of the world's darkest forces, than the pre-fight hooligan mantra, 'Let's go fucking mental, let's go fucking mental'? Finally, right out the other side, there is the slow, eerie 1970s proclamation, 'We are evil, we are evil'.

There is no occult crossover with the humorous song, many of which are found comical by some fans but woundingly offensive by others. Supporters like to think that most of their ditties are quite droll and witty, even when they are not. The sharpness of football fans is one of those strange areas that is consistently both overstated and understated. *When Saturday Comes (the half decent football book)* got it about right:

> 'The results have often been crude, racist and sickening, but also sometimes endearing and funny, and, perhaps more often than some care to admit, an uncomfortable mixture.'

Most football fans would find the following amusing, as it not only reworks a Chelsea classic but also appears to tell an important truth about the Pensioner's fans:

> 'Carefree, wherever we may be,
> We are the nouveau CFC.
> Would you mind sitting down so my wife can see?
> We've been coming here since 2003.'

Chelsea's longer-standing supporters, who have put up with years of yo-yoing between divisions and no silverware are, however, less amused.

Football songs are intended to bring people together and mark them apart, to worship and blaspheme, to build faith and express tribalism, in much the same way as any religion or cult. This was even more so in the past, when the only time the average supporter might hear the tribal anthems and learn the words to new ones was actually at, or around, the match. Occasionally, the words might be conveyed via Match of the Day, often over an embarrassed commentator, but generally one had to be there or know someone who had. The Internet has rather wrecked that close personal link, but the point of the songs, prayers, chants or hymns of all types remains the same: to bind and, hopefully, to alter reality and, in football terms, to help a side to win by 'sucking the ball into the net'. Many supporters believe in the idea that they are a twelfth man driving on the team and affecting the game. Whether one believes that the spells work is largely a question, as in all belief systems, of faith. And faith is what binds the occultist to the churchman to the football fan, although, of course, these categories are not mutually exclusive.

When I find myself in times of trouble

Talismans, scapegoats and the wisdom of elder gods

Since the beginning of their time on this planet human beings have been trying to make sense of their environment and make the odds in favour of survival just that little bit better. Sometimes this involves practical achievable goals such as building a shelter to keep the rain out. At other times it might mean attempting to control, through ritual, magic or prayer, much more difficult and complex things like when the rain comes. Some of those rituals evolved through a chance coincidence of two events occurring simultaneously and a causal link being assumed, others through close observation of natural phenomena. A few are really only allegories, stories to make sense of existence, and acted out each year as a reminder that there is order and pattern to the universe.

The rituals and beliefs behind them provide a framework for viewing the World and offer comfort in difficult times as well as guidelines to possible action. In footballing terms the achievable part in the opening paragraph might be putting an unimaginative clogger at right back. However controlling the timing of attacks, which the defender has to deal with, is to enter a different arena entirely. As with primitive tribes folk footballers rely on their own strength and wits as well as placing faith in their talisman and blame on the scapegoat.

Traditionally a talisman is any object carried for protection or charged with aiding its bearer in the achievement of their ambitions. Examples include gemstones, shells, drawings and virtually any small article, in some cases written words or perfume that attracts a specific force or energy. Footballers and others might slip a talismanic family heirloom into their boots or wear it around their neck but they need not be inanimate. In 1948 Botafogo (of the Brazilian League) adopted a little dog, named Biriba, as their talisman after his presence seemed to bring them victory. The dog was given a win bonus, a gold collar and a reserve player tasted his food whilst another had to sleep under the stand with the canine at night. Things got even more extreme after Biriba, prior to another victory, urinated on one player's leg. In subsequent matches this too became a ritual, all part of the mutt's magic.

Wiccans have a strong belief in sympathetic magic so naturally collect objects which they believe have power and presumably would argue that if Biriba himself was magic then so would what issued from him. The player (Braguinha) no doubt regarded this as taking the piss. In wiccan there is a whole pantheon of symbols relating to all aspects of human behaviour based on planetary system and correspondences of sympathetic magic. The key symbol though is the pentagram (or seal of Solomon). In many societies, religious objects such as a representation of a god or their symbol served. Their inversion, for example an upside down crucifix, became a sign of playing for the other team, whereas a horseshoe the right way up brings luck and offers protection from the devil.

There are many tales as to why horseshoes perform this role but the best known relate to a holy man attempting to 'shoe' the devil with a red hot one. The power of the holy man and his victory over evil is transferred to the object he used to attain that victory, the horseshoe. In reality the actual power emanates from the person originally, whether or not God was acting through them. Heroes from antiquity had this characteristic and courageous fighters would have it assigned to them so that others felt braver and safer around them. Great leaders, warriors and philosophers as well as religious figures from across the belief spectrum have all been said to have talismanic qualities and this is the most common use in modern footballing parlance for Alan Shearer say or David Beckham. What Thierry Henry has in common with Archbishop Desmond Tutu, or indeed Joan of Arc, is not that he is black or French but that he is the person the faithful turn to for help or look to for guidance. Wolves had Steve Bull as a player who performed the role and Steven Gerrard excels at it for Liverpool. These lucky shields are something to cling to in order to turn fortunes around by channelling hope, and unusual balls, to that hero in the faith that they can change the situation with a 'moment of magic'. After all modern footballers are heroes and a hero in Greek mythology was originally a demigod so it shouldn't be all that hard surely?

If the hero fails though someone must be blamed so whether a player succeeds or not can have far reaching consequences for their coach. A study from Cambridge University in July 2006 found that a manager's job and how long he remains in it may just turn on one or two odd bits of fortune or hard luck. The conclusions of the study, which explored the qualities responsible for securing and maintaining high-level jobs concluded that in the end, something as trivial as a key player twisting their ankle in training can be crucial. The survey covered seven thousand individuals over a hundred and thirty year period and, though concentrated on European football, took in Japanese and American managers too. What emerged was the importance of public perception and a so called inverse power law which runs that the longer the time served as manager, the lower the probability of the manager continuing. There is a belief in football that over a season poor decisions for a team or injuries even out across a league but this may not help a coach under fire. The ratio of wins and losses creates thresholds of reputation that determines the length of the manager's time at the top but it is the more recent results that have the greatest effect.

To these factors could be added fan and board's expectations that fluctuate depending on the team. A traditionally successful club might be expected to be quicker on the trigger than others, though quite how this explains the managerial merry go round at Queens Park Rangers is anyone's guess. If however luck can be shown to play a great part by such empirical methods it is only backing up what football fans have known for years. The two most successful managers their clubs' have ever known, Howard Kendall at Everton and Sir Alex Ferguson at Manchester United, both owe their triumphs in a large part to chance. In 1984 and 1990 respectively, with fans and press demanding their dismissal they were fortunate in the early rounds of the FA Cup, to go on to lift that trophy and then to greater things.

The managerial role has evolved quite rapidly and is a relatively new phenomenon with several top sides not appointing an official manager until the late 1930s. The modern concept goes back to Herbert Chapman at Arsenal who was the first, in the 1920s, to fuse the identity of coach, tactician, selector and organiser of transfers as well as other 'off the ball' matters. Prior to Chapman there had been, starting with William Sudell at Preston North End, the idea of a tactician and organiser but once so many responsibilities were put in the hands of a single person they became central to how a club fared. In his book *The Soccer Tribe* Desmond Morris refers to managers as the tribal witch doctors. It is the manager's job 'through sheer strength of personality, and few ritual incantations, to convert a team of cynical, hard bitten professional sportsmen into a group of possessed fanatics.' Like all witch doctors he must be part hypnotist, part psychologist and part sorcerer.' Or as Tim Cahill eloquently said of David Moyes; 'We'd run through walls for our manager.'

Many aspects of management have moved on since Morris wrote his book. There are certificates, courses in sports science and a decent grasp of the principles of nutrition are required but the essential skills of persuasion, judgement and apparent invincibility are still key. As Mark O'Brien wrote in *When Skies Are Grey* it is a matter of selecting the right tyrant to put in charge. These leaders also, quite naturally, became the scapegoat, the one sacrificed if things go wrong. As outlined above it may not be their fault that a club is doing badly but, like the witchdoctor, they must take the blame for failure as well as the plaudits for success. They are the most acceptable sacrifice to the gods, or in today's world the furies represented by the fans and media. Their sacking signifies, in tribal terms, a purging of evil, an opportunity to start afresh and it is hoped that this blood letting will allow the rest of the tribe, or team, to prosper. In more extreme circumstances an even higher sacrifice (that of the board) is required to appease the fanatical faithful.

Scapegoats once could have actually been goats or any other animal, including a person, killed or symbolically slain in order to restore balance. Such ceremonies are found in all human societies and still take place today in modified forms across the world. In ancient Rome on March 14th a man covered in skins was led in procession through the streets, beaten with white sticks and driven from the city. He was taking on all the weight and dead foliage of the old year that had to be cast out before new life could flourish. Similar ceremonies take place across Italy in the 21st century. Other societies were more brutal, and pleasing though the image is of Harry Redknapp being carted up some Peruvian mountain to have his heart ripped out (assuming they could find it), most modern manager scapegoats have it easy. They have a bit of a rough time in the press, a stint as commentator, and then patiently wait for Crystal Palace to come calling. Because when it comes down to it there are fairly few witch doctors, or football managers at a certain level.

In the fifties and sixties the great talismanic club icons emerged whose personalities were locked into their teams and who in a very real sense created the myths and identity for some sides. Danny Blanchflower at Tottenham or Jock Stein at Celtic had alongside responsibility for coaching, transfer activities and tactics, the matter of media relations. This is a position that some are clearly more suited to than others and one that has grown in importance since the middle of the twentieth century with managers out quipping each other. One of the best, in a very competitive field came from Arsene Wenger who said 'everyone thinks they have the prettiest wife at home' after Sir Alex Ferguson suggested Manchester United played nicer football than Arsenal. The manager is in most respects, certain chairman also relish the spotlight, the club's mouthpiece and it is an important role because words carry great power to inspire, invoke, infuriate and influence, they must also soothe, settle, sound sophisticated and, if possible, smart.

Confidence is obviously key because that can be transmitted to others so Brian Clough's proclamation that: 'I wouldn't say I was the best manager in the business. But I was in the top one' is a good start as is nice guy Terry Venables' assertion that 'certain people are for me, certain people are pro me.' Whilst a little understated myth making is also useful as when, after acquiring Ron Yeats, Bill Shankly asked some assembled journalists to 'take a stroll around my new centre half'. On occasion a kind of Zen like dualism is handy when dealing with football's higher mysteries. So it is with Chris Hutchings' comment that 'some of our top players are out injured. That's an excuse, but it's also not an excuse' or Glenn Hoddle's 'I have a number of alternatives, and each one gives me something different.'

This ability to sound wise, represent several positions at once and occasionally come across like a real philosopher grappling with the duality of life is nicely summed up by Francisco Maturana who said after a sound beating that 'every defeat is a victory in itself', a comment supported by John Toshack who opined that 'winning all the time is not necessarily good for the team.' Bertie Mee, former Arsenal coach, took praise to a new realm with 'outside of quality we had other qualities' whilst Joe Royle adopted a kind of Christ like, if slightly confused, sin forgiving role when he said 'I don't blame individuals, I blame myself.' Graham Taylor moved up to the position of a truly omnipotent being when he declared 'it's the only way we can lose, irrespective of the result.'

Giving clear directions is extremely important for the momentum of a club because as Peter Reid said 'in football, if you stand still you go backwards,' which may not be all bad to Dave Sexton who stated that 'the way forwards is backwards.' Gerry Francis was confused, if merciful, when he proclaimed 'it would have killed them off a little bit.' Finally proving that footballers can live on after death is the ghoulish Gordon Lee with his shiny forehead and scary black mackintosh saying, 'even when you're dead, you must never allow yourself just to lie down and be buried.'

There are occasions though when beautiful abstractions, supreme confidence and the intimation of a God-like ability to control the laws of physics give way to brutal honesty. A coach must be bold and provide clarity for their followers. These range from statements of the obvious like Bobby Robson's startling assessment of Michael Owen that 'in a year's time, he's a year older' to Don Howe's shrewd observation of his team's supporters grasp of the game's fundamentals that 'at the end of the day, the Arsenal fans demand that we put eleven players on the pitch.' Franz Beckenbauer was perhaps too dour when he described his German side as 'a good average team' whilst Gerard Houllier was keen to be precise in his use of English when he corrected a journalist by saying 'it was not a mistake, it was a blunder.' Malcolm Allison was more general in his consideration of his team's failings when he acknowledged that 'a lot of hard work went into this defeat.'

Teams need to be encouraged after such setbacks and be given targets such as 'we're going to start the game at nil-nil and go out and try to get some goals' (Bryan Robson) even if they are not actually presented as such, 'I'm not going to make it a target but it's something to aim for' (Steve Coppell). Individual criticism or encouragement needs to be delicately handled as the master of motivation Sir Alex Ferguson displays with his assertion that 'Cole should be scoring from those distances, but I'm not going to single him out.' Dave Basset meanwhile shows that optimism should be boundless yet tempered when he declared 'I honestly believe we can go all the way to Wembley - unless somebody knocks us out.'

If all else fails the witchdoctor manager can fall back on a good mixed metaphor drawing heavily on folk sayings. These will at worse confuse and at best bewilder, either way the players, or hopefully the fans, will be distracted. The strength of these is that they touch on old legends, Terry Butcher accepting that 'the beauty of cup football is that Jack always has a chance of beating Goliath', for example. Some appear to be really magical as evidenced by Mark McGhee's assessment of fellow manager David Jones who 'has this incredible knack of pulling a couple of chickens out of the hat each season,' apparently. Gerry Francis was less fulsome about Jurgen Klinsmann who apparently took to 'English football like a duck out of water' whilst Bruce Rioch revealed his tactics when he said 'we threw our dice into the ring and turned up trumps.' Better perhaps than the spanner thrown on the fire by Bobby Gould or the slightly confused, and clearly saucer less, Terry McDermott observing that 'no-one hands you cups on a plate.' Occasionally the natural order is inverted by that cheerful lord of misrule Craig Brown with his comment that 'the underdogs will start favourites for this match' whilst, for sheer folksy nonsense nothing beats Gianluca Vialli's opinion that 'you must be as strong in March, when the fish are down.'

It would be stretching a point to suggest that these are exactly spells or mantras, particularly the previous selection but some of the coaches' comments are quoted by the faithful and handed down the generations. They become in a real sense a guide to living, a further extension of tribal belonging and expression of identity. The cult of personality attached to the manager and the veneration of their perceived wisdom inspires confidence in both the team and their followers. Footballers are often very quick to proclaim the virtues of a new coach or appear stunned by the power of their character. One of the smugger comments from Arsenal fans around the turn of the century was 'Arsene knows' an all purpose defence that whatever happened it was all down to a cunning plan by Arsene Wenger. On the negative side what a manager says can harm the standing of a club and act like a curse. It will for example be interesting to see if Avram Grant will ever get over Jose Mourinho's assertion that he had the air of a loser about him.

After their retirement the successful ones in the long term become the focus of a kind of ancestor worship, revered totems, sung about in times of crisis, wistfully thought about and almost prayed for. The idea, as mentioned elsewhere is of a once and future king who it is hoped may rise again, though whether this is actually a good idea is being sort of trialled at Derby County with Nigel Clough. The situation is rather different in the short term because when gods are replaced, or great managers leave, it is a time for ruthless sacrifices in order to ensure continuity. In many societies the scapegoat, mentioned above, represented a god, or an old god dying each winter allowing a fresh one to be born in the spring, the Christian resurrection is one take on this legend. In order for this process of rebirth to be complete no physical trace of the old god must be left, temples must be covered or the deity driven from the city. This is pretty close to what Liverpool Football Club did to the man that, in a sense, made them great. Even if he isn't their most successful manager Bill Shankly created the myth of Liverpool, bringing them out of the shadow of the then more successful and better supported Everton and paving the way for two decades of incredible triumphs.

It is paradoxical that Shankly, who once answered a barber's question 'do you want anything off the top' by saying 'Everton' should have spent his declining years feted at Goodison Park and granted access to their training ground whilst Liverpool's was off limits. He was of course adored at Anfield but never allowed admission to boardroom or changing room. There is no evidence that Shankly resented this and, as a realist as well as a visionary, would probably have appreciated the reasons. In the shadow of the mighty it is hard for others to prosper so Bob Paisley at Liverpool was given the freedom from the physical presence of Bill Shankly to build his own, ultimately more successful, sides. This harsh but necessary slaughter of the elder god was a lesson that Manchester United failed to apply to their own legend in residence, Sir Matt Busby, who remained behind the scenes at Old Trafford until his death. The results speak for themselves and it was two decades after Sir Matt retired before Manchester United won anything of note. The lesson in football, as with primitive tribes, is to move on you must kill your idols.

A greater immediacy in football and elsewhere in the modern world demanding faster results and quicker rewards that the goats are dispatched with bewildering speed. Most former managers are players, though it is not always the most successful ones who make the best managers, but still the job requires intelligent analysis, astute observations of your own teams and the opponents' strengths and weakness. There must be studying of footage of your rivals, working on set pieces, gearing up your key stars and delivering Churchillian team-talks. There is so much more but then it is always important to listen to quiet voices near to you. This is what Stuart Pearce did during one of Manchester City's all too frequent runs of comedy form. His seven year old daughter suggested that Pearce kept her cuddly toy Beanie Horse by his side during the match against West Ham and his worries would be over. For a while they were, three points against the Hammers were followed by a good result in the next game. Of course only a loving father could really believe that sort of thing might work but love does tend to blind everyone. What else could explain England manager Glenn Hoddle's faith in healer Eileen Drewery in the 1998 World Cup.

God in the squad

Holy goalies and footballers' faiths

J ose Mourinho affected a certain disdain for common morality whilst at Chelsea saying that 'some clubs are treated as devils, some are treated as angels' but he didn't care how Chelsea were viewed. He is much clearer however about his own position with regard to the universe, 'God, and after God, me.'

Many British football clubs have their origins in organised Christianity or as off shoots of Sunday schools so it would be improper not to make some reference to more established religious practises. Most of the comments made about the occult from prayer and ritual to collective singing and faith apply equally to the Christian religion. A decent case too can even be made that to some people football itself is a religion, or rather a specific team is worshipped and rites observed by followers. The two faiths link with many teams having a club chaplain and others (Barcelona for example) a chapel, whilst St. Mirren are actually named after a proletysing priest. There is however only one team, Queen of the South, which are actually mentioned in the Bible even if they play their football in Dumfries not anywhere near where the Queen of Sheba lived.

Not all teams had a Christian baptism and there are many secular clubs with links to universities and (grammar or public) schools whilst others are the outgrowth of pub teams or, at least, set up after pub meetings. Some, including Sheffield Wednesday, West Bromwich Albion and Preston North End, are the offshoot of another sport, very often cricket teams who wanted a winter game as well. Rarer are those where the change was from another cold weather activity like hockey (Nottingham Forest) or rugby (Bradford City). A decent number began as company sides including Doncaster Rovers, York City and Manchester United all from railway companies though sadly the best named professional works side (Ironopolis of Teeside) have no direct relationship to the current Middlesbrough.

Although football is now big business those teams were just an adjunct of another concern as were their religious rivals. Football was a part of something else, a diversion, rather than an end in and of itself and certainly not the focus of worship on a Sunday that it became. Over a quarter of the teams that have played in the top flight in the last two decades were started by churches including a couple of the most nomadic. Queens Park Rangers were formed 1882 after St. Jude's and Christchurch Rangers merged and played at twenty home venues before settling at Loftus Road in 1917. Bolton acquired the name Wanderers because of their roving ways after breaking with their church origins in 1877. During their homeless period they had a pitch next to a piggery thereby acquiring another nickname, the Trotters.

Other teams with church roots in England include Barnsley, Fulham, Notts County, Aston Villa, Southampton, and, perhaps oddly in view of their strong Jewish connection, Tottenham Hotspur. Grammar school boys from a Bible study group formed them, whilst Everton were originally a football team for the boys of St. Domingo Methodist Church. As with many sides the idea behind their formation was that regular sport might help to curb what today would be known as anti social behaviour in the local area and instil Christian values. Which branch of Christianity remains unclear as despite their Methodist origins and the presence of St. Luke's the Evangelist (Church of England) actually at the corner of Goodison Park, Everton were often regarded as a 'Catholic' team.

This provoked a dilemma for Alan Edge who manages to conflate two issues, football as religion and football in conflict with religion, in his book *Faith of our Fathers*. He has a real crisis of conscience at school, age ten, when he hears that his beloved Liverpool FC had Protestant links which sent his Catholic guilt into overdrive as he realises that:

> 'Our lady was always in blue and white; the school football colours were to become blue and white; the parish priests, the archbishop and the Pope were all blues; probably even our guardian angels were blues.... perhaps it was a sin to support Liverpool and not Everton; maybe a mortal sin or even a sacrilege.'

There are many who think Alan has it about right in that last line but after much fretting and fears of eternal damnation he prays to St. Jude (patron saint of lost causes). His prayer is answered when a famous missionary, priest and friend of the Pope, who happens also to be a Koppite, visits the school. After that he finds lots of red Catholics allowing faith and football to unite.

It would be overstating the case to say that there is an absence of religious sectarianism in Liverpool but there are not the clear cut football related divisions that exist in Scotland between predominantly Protestant sides (Glasgow Rangers, Hearts) and Catholic ones (Celtic and Hibernian). Other clubs such as Dundee United, who like Celtic and Hibernian, were set up by the city's Irish community don't have the same degree of religious baggage attached.

This is just as well as football has developed enough sacred twaddle of its own over the past century with its elders, saints, sacraments and even what amounts to its own liturgy in the series of clichés that surround the game. These are readily spouted by fans, commentators, players and managers and are immediately understood by the initiated whilst leaving outsiders vaguely confused. Beyond football, and possibly street markets, it is unlikely that anyone says, or understands the phrase 'to set out one's stall early doors' for example, or why it's necessary to say 'a big ask' rather than 'asking a lot of someone.' Disturbingly in this parallel faith world the fate of the language is in the hands of Alan Green and other footballing lay preachers.

Some proper priests speak both the real liturgy and the footballing one and actively involve themselves. When Manchester United won the 1999 Champions League with two injury time goals the United chaplain, Rev. John Boyers, confessed to praying in the final seconds of the game. He was humble but determined, and said, 'Lord, if it's part of your intention, we really do need your intervention to win.' That prayer was answered as were, to judge by the number of wildly celebrating priests in 2004's European Championships, those of the Greek Orthodox community. Several Latin American teams involve their holy men much earlier and have priests in as part of the pre match talk.

All of the above would probably disapprove of Robbie Fowler being referred to as God during his first spell at Anfield. In Argentina however things have been taken even further with the establishment of La Iglesia Maradoniana. The first 'Maradonian Church' whose insignia is D10S, from the word for God and Maradona's number ten shirt, started out with a congregation of about fifty now claims 120,000 members, unsurprisingly 1500 of whom are Scottish. These all live AD (after Diego), observe the ten (Maradona inspired) commandments, say special prayers, observe holy days like Maradona's birthday and can even be married to a Maradonian rite. Viewed more broadly the status of the stars as role models is an issue and not, to be fair, something they should have imposed on them. Many players clearly have feet of gold but heads full of clay. Their involvement in drunken fights, sexual depravity or financial greed shows the elevation of players to God like status has many problems, as it says in Exodus 10:4-5 idolatry is forbidden.

There is a book by Mark Roques called *Fields of God* in which the author struggles with the notion that football is the Lord's game because of the greed, cruelty and several of the deadlier sins attached to it. Roques himself describes aspects of football as akin to Canaanite fertility rituals and fans being like ancient tribesman bowing down to rats, frogs, trees and crocodiles. Leaving aside roasting and worship of false idols he does have more compelling arguments for believing that Satan may have a greater hand in football than God. One vignette he relates is about the Serb gangster Zeijko Raznatovic, better known to the world as Arkan. This thug brought success to the team he owned after 1996 (Obilic Belgrade) by literally beating other teams and gassing them in their changing rooms (these worked indirectly as well with Red Star Belgrade getting changed in car park). Tactics pioneered by Uday Hussein in Iraqi on his own Olympic side.

Sir Alex Ferguson has said that football 'becomes a sort of religion in people's minds,' and in a debate on football and religion Anglican Canon Edward Bailey suggested that in modern society people increasingly organise their lives around football the way they once did around religion. He goes on to ponder that 'if it's habitual, it's to do with our identity. Identity is sacred, it's our innermost, deepest self. Isn't that sacred?' He develops the point by citing Buddha to show that religion needn't actually involve God. Two Brazilian researchers (Professors Ricardo dos Santos and Francisco Teixeira) claim that football is almost a secular faith with its own myths and, with games played on a Sunday, in direct competition with the church. They also stress the role that football, as opposed to religion, played in the creation of the Brazilian national identity.

Under such provocation it is understandable that the established church has attempted to fight back. The Vatican, via a consortium of Catholic businessmen, bought an Italian club and also set up its own cup competition between seminaries (the Clericus Cup). This is intended as a demonstration that the game need not necessarily entail match-fixing or diving. It was the idea of Cardinal (and Juventus fan) Tarcisio Bertone. The Clericus Cup's competition slogan is 'a different football is possible' and the rules indeed are. The games are shorter and without yellow or red cards which were replaced by exile to a sin bin (or penalty purgatory) for a specified time. Other aspects of the competition were reassuringly ordinary with the British team put out by a bunch of Croatian priests. More amusingly an overconfident American midfielder said: 'when you love God you can't lose' before going down four nil.

This cup was part of a wider initiative to encourage priests to think of sport as a way of engaging with their flock, but it also raised the question of tribal and religious loyalties conflicting. The competitors organised themselves into national teams, and, as the players warmed up by praying together, their supporters chanted the country's anthem. For Catholics at least this might be solved if, as planned by Bertone, the Vatican had its own side. That may be some time away but the church clearly sees engagement with the world's game as important and recognises the influence football can have on behaviour. Another commentator, Professor Mark Dowd (in *Hallowed be thy Game*), develops the theme about religion/football's capacity to inspire good and evil in people by suggesting that hooligans are the fundamentalists of the game. This conjures up the amusing prospect of the Holte End Intifada at Aston Villa or Tech End Martyrs Brigade (Wrexham).

Islam, like Christianity, has a mixed relationship with football. The 2002 Senegal team prayed to Allah before every match and despite emptying the mosques in the capital Dakar were feted by the city's chief Imam. By the end of the tournament their French coach, Bruno Metsu, converted to Islam. Former world footballer of the year George Weah is a devout Muslim who prays to Allah before every match but elsewhere there are issues. These are (Afghanistan aside) less so to do with the sport itself than the uniforms and symbols around it, most specifically the wearing of imitation shirts. In the first place there are warnings from the prophet that: 'Whosoever emulates a group of people, he is of them' which is of course half the point of football tops. Frederic Kanoute - who once donated £700,000 to save a Mosque in Andalusia- refused to wear a shirt with a gambling firm's logo on it. Other injunctions are also understandable for good Muslims as, for example, kits with breweries for sponsors on might encourage others to sin by taking intoxicants.

Any form of refreshment during a time of fasting is forbidden which put the ironically named Christian Negouai in a difficult position when he was forced to break Ramadan fast to provide a sample for an FA drugs test. There are also concerns about the wearing of red that is considered evil and the squandering of money on such idolatrous and unnecessary items. For as the Qur'an says: 'Verily the spendthrifts are brothers of the Shaytaan and Shaytaan was ungrateful to his Lord.' (Al Isra' 17:27).

This may just offer religious backing for the notion that replica strip wearing fans are going to hell but Peter Howitt is able to quote the Bible in favour of the game. He reminds us that our bodies are temples of the Holy Spirit (1 Corinthians 6:19), so the welcome news is that football (or any exercise) helps us to maintain the splendour of our anatomical shrines. We can also act as God wishes by playing the game in the right spirit. As in all aspects of life we must try and live up to Christian ideals, being the salt and the light in the world (Matthew 5:13–16). This means playing by the rules, encouraging others to do well and behaving with equanimity on the football pitch. In that small way the devout sportsman can influence those he plays with and football can become more than just a game. Mark Roques says: 'In football you see an explosion of spatial possibilities and it's there that you see what I call the glory of God … If you have a secularised world view, you don't see it, it doesn't have that significance.'

As well as having their origins in religion football clubs mimic many of the roles traditionally performed by the church. Children are christened after footballers rather than saints, weddings take place at several grounds and the COOP offers club coloured coffins. Some of the faithful wish to have their ashes spread on the pitch, or at Goodison Park, buried under the penalty spot. Boca Juniors in Argentina sectioned off a bit of cemetery and fans can be buried in club colours on a football stand-shaped lawn reached via a goal-shaped entrance. Hamburg HSV fans have also set up their own specially designated cemetery within earshot of the Nordbank arena as scattering ashes on the pitch is banned in Germany. The club's anthem, Hamburg My Pearl, is sung at every service.

What late Victorian churchman (and nine times FA Cup finalist) Lord Authur Kinnaird might have made of all that is open to conjecture but Peter Lupson, (*Thank God for Football*) quotes Kinnaird as saying. 'I believe that all right-minded people have good reason to thank God for the great progress of this popular national game.' Kinnaird did a fair bit himself to promote the game and shift it from being a largely upper class amateur sport. Football's progress was seen as 'God's work' in another areas too. Anna Connell, daughter of the local rector, wanted to provide activities that would engage local men in hobbies other than alcohol and violence created a team called St. Marks. Later this outfit became Manchester City whose celebrity fans are noted for their temperance and pacifism.

There are some specific players who have a religious bent or devout people who have a footballing one. Despite the alleged fear some of them have of crosses the late Pope John Paul II, follows the strong tradition of Nazarenes in the net. Karol Józef Wojtyła, better known to the world as Pope John Paul II regularly played in goal for both his school and University sides. Whilst Pontiff he found time to bless the marriage of Republic of Ireland international keeper Shay Given. Other holy goalies include two ordained ministers who made it into the England international set up. George Raikes won four full caps and the Rev W Blackmore was selected to play in a match against Wales. Leonard Small was Moderator of the General Assembly and Chaplain to the Queen as well as Scotland international. Church authorities who thought it wasn't quite right for a man of the cloth to be chucking himself about in the mud blocked his career between the sticks.

Sometimes it is the player who chooses the narrow path rather than the broad pitch. Jimmy Allen of Swindon Town refused to play on Sundays whilst Carlos Roa declined to turn up altogether in 1999 because he believed the world was going to end in 2000 and football was getting in the way of his preaching. Brazil's João Leite combined the two roles, as founder of a religious movement and goalkeeper, by setting up the 'Christ's Athletes' movement was once banned from writing religious slogans on his shirt and quipped that 'they can take Christ off my shirt but never from my heart'. Marvin Andrews believes that Christ resides all over his body and that his faith in God has cleared up serious (including career threatening) injuries in record times both at Livingston and Glasgow Rangers. American Adin Brown, who played for Aalesund in the Norwegian Premier League, has been less successful in his faith and had a career plagued by injury and often has trouble regaining full fitness due to his Christian Scientist beliefs which dictate that he cannot use many forms of treatment. Peter Knowles formerly of Wolves might have faced similar problems had he not retired when he became a Jehovah's Witnesses.

A kind of muscular Christianity is common across British football particularly as more players are drawn from strongly religious communities in Africa and elsewhere. Not all of them overtly proclaim their faith in interviews or, as Steven Pienaar in the Premier League and Lucio in the Champions League did, on a t-shirt worn under their team strip. Linvoy Primus believes that there is a correlation between his faith and better football as does Ghana international Sammy Kuffour. Alongside the health benefits of an abstentious religious lifestyle there are sound practical psychological reasons, similar to those covered in the chapter on ritual and superstition, which can aid the conscientious kicker. Top level footballers are under tremendous stress to perform and faith is the rock which many of them cling to. They are possibly also helped to by the memory of the son of God crucified in a fashion that even the harshest tabloid blasting or managerial tongue lashing couldn't compete with.

Erstwhile Coventry City and Hereford stopper David Icke took things to a new level by claiming to actually be the son of God. However as psychiatrist Dr. Heather McKee said at the time 'we have wards full of them'. Icke's revelation occurred at a specially convened press conference at Gatwick Airport where he had just landed with his spiritual advisor, a Canadian by the name of Mari Shawsun. He let it be known that Shawsun would henceforth be referred to as the Daughter of God while his wife was to be called the Spirit of the Angel of God. He chose this moment to predict numerous disasters including the disappearance of Cuba and the Isle of Wight, though oddly not Coventry City's from the top flight of English football where that had been happily ensconced since the 1960s. Icke seemed to vanish himself in the 1990s only to re-emerge this century as a lecturer on highly improbable conspiracy theories.

In contrast to the well established religious beliefs of many players and the rather more outlandish notions of David Ike are the views of British philosopher, and Spurs fan, AJ Ayer. Ayer was closely associated with the British humanist movement and refused to acknowledge the influence of the divine in anything, least of all football. Rational behaviour one supposes as if ever a place might make one despair of the concept of a merciful God then White Hart Lane might be the spot. Rationalist existential philosopher, and Nobel Prize winner, Albert Camus' entire philosophical approach can be summed up by the position of the goalkeeper who is, at once, a part of the team and yet separate. He declared that all he was most certain about on morality and obligations he owed to football. Perhaps this accounts for Camus' brand of existentialism being far more human and less rigid than the Parisian philosophers grouped around John Paul Sartre, a swag bellied bearded goal hanger if ever there was one.

Monty Python once did a sketch about an international football match between German and Greek philosophers which the Greeks win one nil (a headed goal from Socrates). In it Hegal argues that the Greek goal is not real and only a construct whilst Marx insisted it was offside. The nature of football is beautifully revealed in those two reactions, one accepting reality as it is and trying to change it the other living in a completely different reality. To any philosopher who knows football, or the footballer who would be a philosopher, the game offers almost unlimited potential to draw parallels with life and the point of existence.

That is the ultimate problem with football. It is an entertainment that inhabits the dreams of hundreds of millions with tremendous power to alter lives for good or ill. As its influence grows globally there are demands on the modern superstars to use their popularity to some 'positive' purpose. This can be anti racism or awareness of global poverty or even specific diseases or social conditions and is one of things Roques argues in his book. In a strange way this is a return to the roots of many clubs that were set up to encourage young men away from the temptations of drink and sin. Whilst the results could be, at best, described as mixed there are tales of redemption through football even in the modern game and the idea, at least, that there should be a moral framework even if it is often ignored. The mix of idealism and practicality is at the root of the game though because, most times, the side comes first. As the 1970s banner proclaimed Jesus may save but Joe Jordan nets the rebound.

Last with their shorts on
Players' superstitions

ormer France coach Raymond Domenech is a superstitious man and a keen believer that the planets and stars have a profound influence on our behaviour. His team selections were influenced by them and he is quoted as saying: 'When I have a Leo in defence, I've always got my gun ready as I know he's going to want to show off at one moment or another and cost us'. He thinks even less of Scorpios but that didn't stop him selecting Thierry Henry and William Gallas because, in the final analysis, they can play a bit. Domenech is the perfect example of someone whose beliefs are regularly contradicted by reality (in the form of Thierry) yet who would not think of abandoning them. That is the beauty of superstition.

The word derives from the Latin super (above) and stare (to stand), meaning 'standing over' or 'standing in awe of'. Which seems quite apt in a footballing context, when one thinks of a snorting Roy Keane above the prostrate body of a clattered forward or Southampton fans bowing down to Matthew Le Tissier. In its more traditional meaning, the derivation points to an unreasonable or excessive belief in, or fear of, what might happen if certain rituals are not observed. It also involves a kind of magical thinking including the notion that the manipulation of effigies or symbols can cause changes to occur in whatever is represented by that symbol. A sort of irrational link between cause and effect has been revealed in a number of studies pinpointing that what top athletes (and other highly competitive people) are after is a suggestion that they are in control in challenging situations.

The multimillionaires of the Premier League will no doubt be delighted to learn that their 'superstitious' responses to uncertainty were first documented by BF Skinner in 1948, amongst pigeons. This isn't to suggest that birds have lucky shin pads, listen to Beyonce or any of the other interesting rituals revealed below but rather that, when confronted with unpredictable rewards (time of food arrival or not), pigeons adopt certain behaviour patterns. According to the *Journal of Sport Behaviour* *(Vol 31 no 2)*: 'Skinner suggested that these behaviours were a result of the pigeons' chance actions being paired unintentionally with the reinforcement [of being given food], which seemed to give the pigeon an illusion of control over the food presentation.'

A logical extrapolation of this could mean that Cristiano Ronaldo has a brain similar to a feral pigeon on account on of a ritual he picked up at Manchester United. The Portugal star got his hair cut at the same Wilmslow barbers before every home match because he scored after the first time he did it. Appearance-related rituals are very common, as are the use of fetishes, pre-match behaviour quirks and prayer, actions which are 'repetitive, formal, sequential, distinct from technical performance and which the athletes believe to be powerful in controlling luck or other external factors' (Bleak & Frederick, 1998). As the game is more broadly reported, so are the various quirks and foibles of the stars. This is unsurprising because, paradoxically, in a world where a player's every comment is worked over for hidden meaning, confessing to a few peculiar pre-match rituals is the most humdrum, non-controversial and human thing they can do. Even if some of those harmless superstitions go right to the core of pagan belief systems.

Before exploring the origins of some practises it is worth stressing that there are many 'ordinary' relaxation techniques or focusing strategies, which have been proven to boost performance. Both they and the more outlandish rituals are attempts to improve a player's ability, although one set is more firmly in the science camp than the other. The former can include taking deep breaths, visualisation, relaxing to music, and repetitive physical actions and practices like shooting at the goal to get in the mood. In contrast, the latter may be represented by taking deep breaths, visualisation, relaxing to music, and repetitive physical actions and practices like deliberately not shooting at the goal for fear of 'wasting a real one', to get a Gary Lineker in the mood.

Coming from an opposite angle, Peter Schmeichel insisted on parrying exactly one hundred shots before each match. The distinction comes when a routine takes on a magical aspect, and the notion that a person can influence an outcome over which they have no control. Unsurprisingly, this has led sports psychologist Keith Power to observe that players 'have to learn to distinguish between superstitions and rituals'.

Goalkeeper David James, who is advised by Power, is bright enough to see the absurdity of it all, yet also the deep necessity:

'Many footballers have an obsessive routine that goes way beyond normal. Mine used to begin the Friday night before a game and continue right through to the full-time whistle the following day. It was a ritual so complex it could fill a page. It was made up of things like going into the urinals, waiting until they were empty and spitting on the wall, or not speaking to anyone. I saw it as preparation – mental machinery. Every ritual represented a cog in the machine and at the end of it came the performance. And the performance had to justify the process. That was the pressure. I was in this mad little world where as long as I did everything in the right order then anything could be achieved. Dangerous thinking, that is.'

He may be even more alarmed to know that, according to Scott *(Discoverie of Witchcraft, 1584)*, to 'unbewitch the bewitched, you must spet into the pissepot, where you have made water'. In the fourth century Pliny, in his Natural History, also mentions this approvingly as a sure way of lifting a curse. Fellow shot stopper Sergio Goycochea of Argentina urinated on pitches ahead of penalty shoot-outs. This started as a call of nature against Yugoslavia in the 1990 World Cup quarter final, but after that initial success it went on to become a regular thing. Again, Sergio would probably be surprised to learn that his peeing antics were employed in the Highlands on doorposts (not goals) to keep the fairies away from women about to give birth.

John Terry, like James, enjoys a pee in the same urinal before home games, wears the same 'lucky' shin pads, and plays the same music and parks in the same spot. He also puts three strands of tape around his legs. None of this makes him a sufferer of obsessive compulsive disorder; these are just his mental preparations. Then again, his use of a fetish (the shin pads), sacred music (R&B is after all based on tribal rhythms) and numerical symbolism (three being a lucky number) might make him the wicked witch of the West Stand.

Terry appears to have selected his own pattern of beliefs but Keith Power observes that many superstitions are down to football's cultural heritage and are self-perpetuating: 'A superstitious manager may pass these on to his team. When they become coaches, the players pass it on again.' Jack Charlton had 'lucky' routes to games when he was manager of Ireland, and his former boss Don Revie made the team walk the last two miles to away fixtures after this once happened by accident and they won. A similar thing occurred with Sven-Göran Eriksson at Lazio when the team bus was diverted and the side subsequently won. The same route to Rome Airport has been taken since. For some, however, the preparation starts at home. David Beckham allegedly arranges his drink cans to face the same way in the fridge door, and Paul Gascoigne insisted on hanging all the towels a certain fashion.

It only takes a quick wiggle around a defender to jump from Paul Gascoigne to one of the more prevalent areas of superstition in soccer: food. One survey for the Premier League sponsors claimed that 40% of fans who buy a pie at half time do so as a superstitious ritual. This is probably a rare case of greed, hunger and boredom masquerading as ritual but many players have pre-match sacred meals, Alan Shearer's chicken and beans, for example. Billy Bremner (former captain of Leeds United and Scotland) shared Shearer's taste for beans and was always careful to finish his meal, although he may not have known of the belief amongst Scottish fishermen that leaving food or giving it away meant that the luck went with it. In the case of the fishermen, this meant the catch; with footballers, it might be a goal or a tackle.

With the advent of stricter dietary control, players' lucky foods and pre-match meals (which for former England international Jimmy Greaves included a roast dinner with custard covered dessert) now tends to manifest itself through what might politely be termed 'uses of bubble gum'. These include chewing the same piece throughout a game or rolling the gum into a ball and attempting to kick it. A successful contact means a good game but, if the player misses, bad luck will follow.

Rio Ferdinand pours water down his face in the tunnel before he enters the field. He is probably just doing it to wake himself up as he claims, and not indulging in a traditional rainmaking rite as outlined the 1486 classic on witchcraft, the Malleus Maleficarum, particularly as a slippery pitch rarely helps defenders. Sometimes Rio splashes his team mates too but they should think themselves fortunate that they don't play alongside Shaun Derry who, whilst at Leeds, forced himself into a pre match-vomit, in what is clearly a purging ritual of sorts.

Members of the nineteen sixties Leeds side feared they would suffer bad luck if they did not emerge from the tunnel in a precise order, with star player Jack Charlton bringing up the rear. He passed up the captaincy because of this, just as Paul Ince did decades later. Ince also waited until he'd left the tunnel before putting his shirt on, a practice he has thankfully given up since entering management. Fortunately, Bobby Moore, who insisted on being the last player to put his shorts on, was always enough of a gentleman to do that in the changing rooms.

Changing rooms are the most intense places for ritualism. Here, there are rigidly observed procedures involving lucky shoes, socks and even laces, the breaking of which can mean misfortune. If their laces come undone, some players walk nine paces (three times three - a Wiccan magic number) before tying them, in order to avert trouble. Doing up boots can therefore become a bit of an ordeal, with players lacing and unlacing them many times before the game, and then only after the serious business of putting the boots on has been attended to. Many go back further to the sock, always putting the left one on before the right. Or vice versa, as there is disagreement as to which brings good luck. To some, putting the left boot on first is a sign of evil to come; for others it is the opposite. All agree, however, that spitting into the right boot before putting it on is a sure way of breaking a curse. Whether it works when you rub whisky on it, as one player used to do, is less well established. That ritual has aspects of a classic votive offering of something valuable, similar to smashing champagne at the launch of a ship, as well as the anointing of a hero.

There are decent historical precedents for Lazio fan and player Paolo Di Canio's custom of putting his left shin pad on first. In the Roman Empire, the left side was considered lucky, except when entering a home. By the Middle Ages, however, the left side tended to be associated with adversity. Interestingly, this luck was transferable and the origins of 'by the left, quick march' meant no mercy for the enemy, so players putting their left boot on first could be transferring the ill luck to their opponents. Misfortune, too, awaits those who accidentally place their right foot into a left shoe; in the Middle Ages, this was thought to leave the hapless wearer vulnerable to witchcraft.

Many players prefer to play in boots that are well broken in. In 1908, when striker George Hedley played for Wolverhampton Wanderers, he scored against Newcastle and split one of his favourite boots. Despite being offered a new pair, Hedley saw the game to completion wearing the tattered boot. He had them patched up at least seventeen times before eventually, and somewhat reluctantly, parting with them. Ian Rush insisted on soaking his new (sponsored) boots at every match after a game with Luton when he did this and went on to score five goals in the game, insisting that they were too dry 'unchristened'. Frank Lampard is one of a number of players who go to the other extreme and throw their boots away after a bad game. Lampard doesn't take the extra precaution of burning them, however, as is practised in some areas to prevent fairies abducting the owner's children.

Another footwear superstition that has faded with the decline of mining in the UK and, more importantly, the number of players who came from pit districts, is the old belief that boots fallen on their side mean bad luck. Colliers would be reluctant to work if they saw their boots had toppled over, as this was seen as a premonition of disaster. Sterile, rodent-free homes and stadia have seen off the idea that a mouse gnawing on footwear spells disaster. New superstitions have arrived to replace them, however. For example, some players remove logos from their boots to get an all-black appearance. This represents a unity of purpose or maybe an anti-corporate gesture from a section of society noted for their dislike of labels. Manufacturers are aware of this practice and incorporate weaknesses such as hidden seams that tear easily once the company's symbol is taken off.

Symbols and crests are mentioned elsewhere in this book, and players often carry their own lucky icon, coin, or even herbs, for good fortune, inside their boots or otherwise on their person. This coin carrying should not be confused with an early football rule which stipulated that players must carry a half crown coin in each hand to prevent open handed shoving. Silver generally is a popular choice as this protects from malignant glances (likely at a game) and werewolves (less so). There is a belief that touch can transfer magic from the sacred object to the person. At the extreme end of this scale are examples of healing by touch, most notably scrofula, which it was thought could be cured by a sovereign's hand. Then there is the luck attached to stroking a cat, donkey, mole or virgin, though those are difficult to hide in a boot and the latter are rarely found near Premier League footballers. Whether the Liverpool team have any of the above in mind when they touch the Liverbird in the tunnel at Anfield is unknown.

This traditional touching of talismans or protective emblems to ward off evil is as old as religion itself, whether the Christian crucifix or the much more ancient pentagram. The 1994 Romanian manager, Anghel Iordanescu, brandished his crucifix and kissed his book of Romanian saints during matches and also refused to let the team bus reverse. Elsewhere in Romania, fans of top flight side Arges Pitesti once staged a cat's funeral and roasted a chicken on the field for good fortune. All of which makes wearing underwear backwards (Adrian Mutu) or the entire 1998 team bleaching their hair in a bid to break a jinx placed on them by a senior figure in the Romanian Orthodox Church seem quite humdrum.

Hair magic is not restricted to the Carpathians, as a glance at the English League will tell you. This divides into three main areas. The dyeing of hair (or otherwise adopting a strange style) for luck is fairly widespread, and allied to the refusal to shave or cut hair. The converse of this are players who cut their hair to change their fortune, such as Gary Lineker, or those who believe that a shaved head is more intimidating and signals a new beginning or statement of intent by an under performing player. Not cutting hair or shaving during a successful cup run was more common in the shaggier 1970s, when cavemen elevens frequently contested the finals. The cutting of hair as a sign of weakness has biblical roots in the story of Samson who lost his strength when Delilah chopped off his mane. Certain religions today (Rastafarianism to name one) regard hair as sacred and certainly there are those in the occult community who are very careful about the disposal of hair in case it is used as a magical weapon against its former host.

This belief is particularly strong in Turkey, which is perhaps to be expected in a country where Fenerbahce debutantes have sheep's blood smeared on their socks before their first game. Britain has even more disturbing sock folklore; Matt Le Tissier confessed to wearing ones bearing an image of the demon known as Mr. Blobby under his kit for months. He eventually stopped after a four-match losing streak, deciding they had 'lost their blobby magic'. Others are swifter to act, and change shirts at half time if things are not going well or in Gary Neville's case keep wearing belts, shoes and aftershave if he has been on a winning run. He is the first to recognise the absurdity of having worked all his life to be a professional footballer then letting everything rest on choice of cologne. Carlos Bilardo, the ex-Argentina coach, relied on a lucky tie he wore throughout the 1986 and 1990 World Cup tournaments, whilst the same particularly battered suit was worn by a Brazilian trainer for their campaigns in the 1950s.

The above examples are really just a snapshot of some of foibles of professional players that cross over from pre-match practices into the world of magic. With music, which serves a number of functions in the modern game, the dividing lines are even more blurred. 'Music therapy' makes claims to provide a relaxing, positive stimulus for mood change and stress reduction. It promotes muscular action, and the right melody can improve the heart rate and lower blood pressure. Ideal, then, for the manager who has just watched his team fall behind after having been two goals up. The ability of music to improve concentration might be handy for goalkeepers and penalty takers alike, while spikier tunes could motivate a sluggish midfield. These are all sound physical or psychological reasons for using it, but alongside the practical reasons –

distraction, heightening emotion and the calming of nerves – are ritual aspects to do with association and expectation. Private and public tunes are also used in different ways before a game.

Music acts as a prelude to religious events, whether it is part of a high Mass or voodoo drumming; and football teams always come out to a rousing chorus. Its purpose is interpreted widely but the general idea is to pump up the home team, intimidate the away side and drive the fans to a state of extreme excitement ahead of the coming spectacle. The practice started in the 1960s and some clubs have kept the same tunes ever since (Liquidator at Chelsea for example). Others are versions of fans' favourites (Bubbles at West Ham), reworked pop 'classics' (Hi Ho Wolverhampton at Molyneux) or songs with a local connection (Man United's use of Dirty Old Town). Several clubs go for pumping newer hits, more classical heart movers (Carman Buranda at Sunderland) or even TV theme tunes (Tranmere Rovers' inexplicable use of the theme from The Rockford Files).

Over time, the power of the music and its association will transport the fan to another place whenever they hear it. When they listen to particular tunes, footballers are using music in much the same way as occultists do, as a means of entering an altered state, by drawing associations from the song, whether from their own life or those they attribute to the music itself. The song may not actually be a player's favourite – John Terry prefers Usher before a match, but his top track is by Luther Vandross. He is not alone; German international Moritz Volz has noted what he calls 'the hoodies controlling the stereo' and the prevalence of R&B in British changing rooms. However, Volz does concede that this might be preferable to the death metal favoured by a couple of goalkeepers he knows.

In a 2003 survey of pre-match anthems, Eminem came top with U2 second. Music psychologist Neil Todd, who conducted the survey, explained the results:

> 'Eminem's music may play a role rather like the Haka – the New Zealand rugby team's pre-match tradition – in helping players reach an aroused competitive state.'

Like the earlier Eye of the Tiger, the theme from Rocky, the music is not only powerful but has an inspirational message concerning overcoming great odds. U2's music works in a different way. By being lively and positive, it induces a sense of euphoria by activating the brain's dopamine system. According to Todd, 'the release of adrenaline prior to a match has the additional effect of raising the heart rate, helping prepare the body for a game'.

Mostly, footballers use the music psychologically, to enter a different mental state. Their choice of sounds ranges from the alarming to the predictable and beyond (Martin Keown chose Simply the Best). There may be a slight element of superstition to this, but others choose tunes that are more to do with accessing magic by association, so playing a particular song at a specific time becomes like lacing their boots a certain way. Former Everton manager Howard Kendall put on Bruce Springsteen and the Christians before every cup game in 1985. Unfortunately, the Christians tape was misplaced before the final and Everton lost to Manchester United. As inspiring as much of Springsteen's and the Christians work is, it was less about the tunes themselves that became important but the order they were played in as part of a psychological build up.

Some cultures use music as a protection against evil, and the relationship between tunes and trances is an extremely close one, with music used in possession rituals practiced across the world by shamans, mediums and exorcists. The shaman, Howard Kendall in this instance, is creating a ritual that includes music, in order for journeys into other worlds to be undertaken. As Norman M. Weinberger, writing in Scientific American, put it: 'music has enormous power to cause emotion to well up within us. These compelling, often overwhelming feelings colour our moods, affect our perceptions and can alter our behaviour.' He was explaining the potency of music and providing a rational support for the seemingly irrational need to play the Sex Pistols (thank you Stuart Pearce) before a big game.

Sex itself before a match is mentioned far less by footballers than other athletes, although former manager of Spurs and Arsenal Terry Neil held a sweepstake as to who had sex nearest to kick off (the winner clocked in at 2.55). Other players share the popular superstition that abstinence can aid concentration. In Latin America this concept (concentraçaõ) is taken seriously with Brazilian teams in particular kept away from alcohol and women. Elsewhere in the game, male fans in Uganda cover their balls in order that an opponent may miss a penalty, and Italians do much the same to ward off the evil eye, jinx or bogey. The superstitious 'protection' this affords has its roots in pre-Christian times and, ironically, predates the term 'bogey' itself, which appears to come from when Christianity supplanted older religions and the gods of the previous era become the goblins and demons in the next. In the case of Everton, Satan's ambassador was Les Ferdinand who by 2000 had scored thirteen goals in fourteen games against them. After that, he appeared to sign to a new team deliberately just to stay in the Premiership and frighten them.

Bogey players or teams are frequently cited in football, and FIFA notes some unlikely, against-all-form successes: Uruguay over Brazil; the USA over Mexico; even Northern Ireland's better than expected run-ins with Spain. For a team or player to be a true bogey, they have to inspire an irrational fear against logic and form, hence Les Ferdinand but as Kevin Pullein in the *Guardian* has noted:

> 'There is a widespread belief in football that certain teams will always play well against others, irrespective of their form or league position. But the bogey team is as much a figment of our imaginations as the bogeyman. Past results in a fixture have no influence over future happenings. The teams who seem to have some sort of spell over their opponents have simply been lucky most of the time.'

Professor Richard Wiseman rather spoils the randomness of this by proving to his satisfaction that some people are actually luckier than others, or at least more open to good fortune. He gathered a group together and asked them to count some photographs in a newspaper. Wiseman noticed that the people who thought of themselves as generally lucky tended to spot the huge adverts that said, 'stop counting photos and demand your prize money from the experimenter.' Those whose approach to life was more Eeeyoreish tended not to.

Against this background of irrationality, it is perhaps ironic that the one thing most often referred to as magic, the physio's sponge, is the one place there is no room for mumbo jumbo in the modern game. To help with their metatarsal, professionals do not routinely use bread made on Good Friday, red thread, a hangman's rope, grass from a churchyard, lizards, mandrakes, spiders' webs, frogs or crosses. Folk cures for common injuries include passing back and forth beneath a natural bramble loop for a hernia, and egg yolks and wood to aid broken bones. That said, Darius Vassell did injure himself while attempting DIY surgery on a blood blister under the toenail on his big toe, using a power drill to drain the wound. This is classic blood-letting, used since ancient Greece to balance the body's 'humours', but normally a qualified person working under sterile conditions would do the trick, or at least a leech, and there are no shortage of those around professional footballers.

Superstition or folk medicine is rarely applied when it comes to actual injuries but it is employed to ward them off, particularly in Africa where amulets and protection charms are common. To suggest that this is all in the mind overlooks the incredible power the mind has over the body. There is the famous example of goalkeeper Bert Trautmann, who played on with a broken neck to help his team Manchester City win the 1956 FA Cup final against Birmingham City. Trautmann confessed to blurred vision afterwards but it wasn't until two days later that he realised the extent of his injuries and that he was lucky to be alive. Clearly, this demonstrates graphically the power of mind over matter and therefore the possibility of mentally altering the outcome of what is, after all, a physical activity. Even if the power of superstition is all mental for some the magic rituals take on astonishing intensity.

Their primary function appears to be that of stress relief, with the actual performance really dependent on training, confidence and physical condition. In one study, confidence levels fed back into the likely success of the ritual, which is about taking (or appearing to take) control of a situation. Superstitions cause athletes to experience less anxiety than they would if they did nothing, so, when a ritual appears to work, it is replayed over and over. This takes us back to the pigeons, and mankind's first faltering steps towards understanding cause and effect where the use of magical thinking is an attempt to stack the odds in favour of survival. In the end, what actually matters is the ritual, not the tradition it belongs to, and the rituals are as individual as the players themselves, so the modern occult ritual or footballers' pre-match shenanigans are equally sacred because they work for the practitioner.

Do they really work? Major studies by sports psychologists have produced inconclusive results. It seems that there is definitely a physical benefit in terms of relaxation, but whether the player is lifted appears to depend on confidence levels, social background and religious belief. Like a placebo medicine, its power is in the mind and, in any evenly matched contest, the extra self-confidence and control of worries engendered by a successful ritual are likely to mean a favourable outcome. Psychologist Willi Railo reckons that 'the psychological difference decides whether you win or lose' whilst Dutch psychologist Willem Wagenaar, estimated that only a small proportion of results could be attributed to individual skill alone. Football teams are not always evenly matched and one player's brilliance is not always enough but, as the old lady said whilst peeing in the sea, or John Terry in his lucky urinal, every little helps.

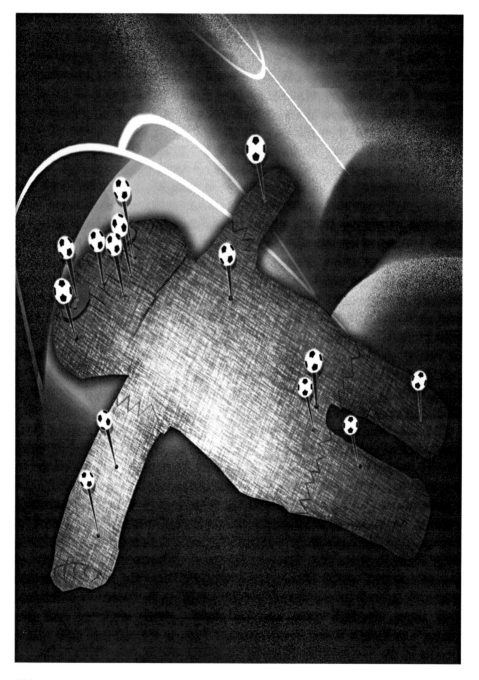

I'll put a spell on you

Witchcraft, voodoo and juju

O n September 16th 2008 the Associated Press news agency ran a report that headlined Witchcraft sparks deadly football riot. Thirteen people died in the disturbances in Butembo, eastern Congo, which were reportedly caused after accusations that a player was using witchcraft. Most of the dead and injured were children and teenagers crushed in a stampede to exit the ground after the local derby between Socozaki and Nyuki System. Ten years earlier *The Independent* reported allegations that wizards had conjured up lightning that killed off an entire team. This happened in Kinshasa (Democratic Republic of Congo) where a freak blast of lightning struck the pitch killing one side whilst the home team were left completely untouched. In a similar, though less deadly incident in South Africa over the same weekend, six players from a local side were hurt when lightning struck the playing field during a thunderstorm. A likelier explanation is that the teams were affected differently because of the type of studs they were wearing with metal ones carrying the deadly charge, nevertheless the popular instinctive reaction was to blame the juju men.

Voodoo, juju, obeah, sorcery, black arts or necromancy, in a sense this is the subject that the rest of the book has been doing step overs around because whatever the tribal roots of the game, however clear the ritualistic parallels or pagan the origins of players' superstitions and no matter how close the crossover in prayers, chants and use of symbols shared by football and the occult; this is the real deal. It is the direct invoking of external forces in an attempt to influence the game by scaring or harassing the opposition. It is also a problem that some national football federations are being forced to recognize.

In November 2004 the Tanzania Football Federation imposed fines on the two main football clubs in the country, Yanga and Simba, after concluding that both had performed spells before a crucial championship deciding derby game. A newspaper even published pictures showing fans of each team burying unknown substances in the pitch on the eve of the match. Whatever forces were invoked they appear to have cancelled each other out as the match ended goalless. As did the previous match when Simba players broke eggs and cast powders onto the pitch but were countered by Yanga urinating on the turf. Both sides were fined for these actions but the practises are so widespread that former Simba official, Kassim Dewji, claimed he was forced out of the club because he believed in coaching and fitness not hoodoo and jinxes. He also claimed that some other officials used sorcery to make money. Even within the ranks of the Tanzanian Football Federation there is some disagreement as one insider claimed that the TFF themselves employed a witchdoctor in a qualifier against Kenya. The Tanzanians lost and coach Mwina Kaduguda claimed that this was because the players' fees had been spent on a juju man, which unsettled the team. The response to this was the compromise that future games would only involve volunteer sorcerers.

This tactic has already been adopted by Kenya who have a witchdoctor talisman, a Mr Isaac Juma Onyango. Mr Onyango has all over body paint, carries a hollowed gourd and dances throughout the full ninety minutes of his team's home games. The moves become more frantic for every goal scored and his presence inspires other fans and players. This all comes at some cost to Mr Onyango because he has to travel nearly a hundred miles to Nairobi, buy his own paint and pay someone to shave him then do the decorating. After being painted he doesn't speak to anyone, abstains from sex and concentrates hard on the game. At least, after a novel 'shirt' sponsorship deal, he no longer has to pay for his transport because he has the bus company name decorating his body.

In 2003 an international between Uganda and Rwanda was interrupted in the second half when the Rwandan goalkeeper lit an amulet in his goal. Officials ignored this but the outraged Ugandans fought their way into the net and made off with the fetish. At this point a kind of Benny Hill chase scene occurred involving both teams, officials and policemen. Ten minutes later the Rwandans retrieved it and calmness prevailed until the goalie lit it again and the whole stadium erupted with both sides brawling in the goalmouth. Astonishingly the match was eventually completed with Rwanda winning one nil. In his book *Elephants, Lions and Eagles* Filippo Ricci describes a market in Mali where honjon items are openly sold. Three quid will get you an elephant's tooth for your sock, thought useful for goalkeepers on the grounds that such a huge beast would fill the goalmouth. It is slightly more for a monkey head and a tenner for a caiman's.

In 1984 more than one hundred fétisheurs stayed with the Ivoirian national team at their hotel during the African Nations Cup. Amongst the rituals they recommended was for each player to take a bath in water treated with various potions before being asked to make a wish in the ear of a pigeon. Just under a decade later a new Ivory Coast squad rose to footballing prominence but again failed to fulfil its potential and then there was a gap of twelve years before the emergence of the current highly talented team. Some believe that necromancy lies at the heart of this. In the early 1990s the then sports minister had enlisted a supporting cast of fétisheurs or juju men to give the Ivoirians a supernatural advantage against Ghana. This may have been a good idea as far as getting the right result went but not paying the sorcerers afterwards could be considered foolish because the unpaid necromancers hexed their own team. What might, in another context, be referred to as trades dispute rumbled on for a decade until defence minister, Moise Lida Kouassi, made amends through money and gin and Ivory Coast made in to the World Cup in Germany in 2006.

How much the ritual slaughtering of chickens before the crucial qualifier against Cameroon helped as well is a matter for debate but the recent success of the Ivory Coast team and the rise to superstardom of Didier Drogba in particular has had many positive effects. These include uniting the country around a shared passion and providing a focus for the disparate groups within it. The president is proud of the support his regime has given the team but is quieter about other elements of the Mighty Elephant's following. These include witch doctors that still scatter charms on the field or smear the goalposts with magic ointments to keep the ball out. Ivory Coast player Didier Zokora joked in the recent tournament about putting a hex on Michael Essien before going onto explain that 'Voodoo is very big. It's a lucky charm. You might take some soil and charm each player. You put it in a bag for every game. If you win, you think, OK, it's good.' The logic behind this ritual is clearly the same that operates for English players and their superstitions about lucky shinpads or laces but Zokora is saying it with the weight of conscious occult tradition to back him up. In the end it may just be cultural differences between the more individualistic

British, where people make up their own rituals, and the more collective African identity and tradition of juju.

Many in the African game though are strident in their opposition to the use of magic in football. At the 2008 African Cup of Nations one official from the Confederation of African Football said that. 'We are no more willing to see witch doctors on the pitch than cannibals at the concession stands.' Delightful though that image is he is not alone and the Football Association of Zambia (FAZ) is one of the more militant in refuting the influence of diabolism in the game. They issued a statement claiming that Zambia is a Christian nation that holds Jesus superior to juju. A BBC reporter who intimated that Zambia was one of a number of nations that employed the so-called wisemen prompted this. Zambia's unambiguous response was in marked contrast to that of other associations in the report about the 2002 Africa Cup which included Mali, Ghana, Nigeria, Burkina Faso, Togo, Ivory Coast, Congo and Cameroon. Cameroon however has subsequently banned all shamanistic team advisors from playing any role. This decision may well be connected to the 2002 semi-final (between Mali and Cameroon) when the German coach of the Indomitable Lions, Winfried Schafer, was arrested for placing a magic charm on the pitch before the match.

Whether this totem was akin to the one a Nigerian FA official removed from beneath the nets at Lagos in 2000 is unclear. That item, which had been placed in the back of the opposition Senegal goal, was removed with fifteen minutes to go by angry Nigerian officials. At this point Nigeria were losing one nil yet went on to win two one the 'magic' goal protection having been taken away. As Africa changes and African football takes a higher profile it is likely that there will be a decline in such overt activities. Kwabena Ofori, the president of Capital Sports FC, a second-division Ghanaian outfit says juju practices are dying out. 'Players who think they may have a broken bone know they have to go and have it x-rayed at a hospital, not wrapped by a traditional healer.' Ghana's Ministry of Education and Sports also recently turned down the offer of help from the self styled queen of all witches of Ghana's Nzemaland region. The sorceress promised spiritual support and to ward off all evil in return for a trip to the World Cup in 2006.

As part of the artistic and cultural programme for that competition Oliver Becker made 'Kick the Lion - Soccer and Magic in Africa'. It is an exploration of the power of myth and hope in football plus the outcomes of games being down to moments of magic, though in this case the magic has little to do with close ball control and slipping a defender. The documentary explores the world of juju and addresses key issues such as how a goalkeeper can draw additional strength from a monkey's paw or the efficacy of zebra's hoof or the fat of a lion on a strikers' accuracy. These are serious matters and clubs are prepared to invest scarce resources in cat fat. Becker observes 'some teams spend so much money on juju that they may be unable to afford travelling to away games.' The money though is for the shaman because the actual materials for rituals might be quite cheap. Pig's blood for example, which is used to smear in rivals' changing rooms or a spare pair of goalkeeping gloves to hang on the net. Parts of animals or plants can also be burned near the goal or strewn there in the form of magic powder. Other materials present more of a challenge as not only are cows relatively expensive but burying one alive on the field in front of the opposition goal as stipulated in one ritual raises all kinds of logistical issues. The point of this beef burial is to suck the power out of one's opponents; however it may be all in vain if they adopt one of a number of avoidance tactics. These can be relatively simple such as altering the way the pitch is approached or entering the field backwards.

Becker's documentary concentrated on Ghana and even if (officially) that country has stopped using juju there is nothing to prevent supporters carrying out their own ceremonies. Becker, quoted in National Geographic News, states that it is safe to assume such practices go on, though less so than in the past. 'Traditional medicine and religion play an important role in most African societies,' and as 'soccer is by far the number one sport in Africa, so it's logical that traditional beliefs would also play an important role in soccer.' So in the 2008 African Cup of Nations opening match between Ghana and Guinea, *The Guardian* reported 'several Ghana fans carried a juju pot containing leaves and liquid in order to scare away all devils, while churchgoers went to their Sunday service bedecked in the country's red, gold and green for a cleansing ceremony designed to inspire total victory'. One South African mushonga drew a nice contrast between the likely efficacy of one form of prayer over the other. After claiming that many footballers employed his services he continued 'most people are afraid to admit they practice my kind of rituals because they go to church on Sundays. They worship God or pray for good luck, but that doesn't work – because sport is a game and God is not a gambler! God is there for us all. He can't protect one team and leave the others alone! That's why you need a mushonga like me.'

Belief in ancient gods and the spirit world is still widespread across Africa and it is not that unusual for football teams to employ a witchdoctor or for matches to begin with a team ritual. These might be a collective prayer or huddle or might be a little more unusual, the slaughter of a white cockerel in the goalmouth for example. Pure mumbo jumbo of course and you'd never catch sensible Europeans doing such things at crucial moments, to say win the World Cup in 1998. Apparently the wrist bands clearly sported by the French side were magically prepared by West African witchdoctor Aguib Sosso to ward off the evil spirits. An extra special pair was made for Zinedine Zidane who might have benefited from a magic headband in the competition nearly a decade later.

Then there are the Romanians whose football chiefs in the run up to Euro 2004 considered using a witch to put a spell on a rival team. Mircea Sandu, president of the Romanian Football Federation, claims they successfully did the same thing to Peter Schmeichel in a similar qualifying match in the late 1980s. This was after coming under immense pressure from the then government which threatened the entire federation with dismissal if a game against Denmark was lost. These were of course difficult times for the Ceausescu regime in Bucharest and it was hoped victory in the crucial qualifier in November 1989 might distract the masses. Under pressure from the atheist regime Sandu replied in a very strange way. He hired a witch to put a spell on the Danish goalkeeper. The witch arrived at the stadium an hour before kick off and performed her ritual, which seemed to work very well as Romania won 3-1 and qualified for the following year's World Cup. It did nothing to help the Ceausescu's though but clearly increased the confidence of Romanian witches who, incensed that Swiss referee Urs Meier played five minutes of injury time allowing the opposition to equalise, cursed Meier so he'd lose the power to whistle. Later in the quarter-finals of the same competition Meier (or Urs Hole to the British press) disallowed an English goal and needed police protection after the game. Since then he may have whistled but always a lower level of the football pyramid. More recently, in 2008, fear that Bulgaria's Defence Minister might cast a bad spell over the team by placing Bulgarian turf on the Farul stadium in Bucharest resulted in him being banned from the ground.

In Latin America a little light voodoo might be considered tame on a continent prepared to go to war over a disputed football game (Honduras and El Salvador) or murder a defender (Columbia) for failing at a World Cup. Even successful sides are prepared to call on help though and since 1970 (when it was started by Rivelino) Brazilian players have cast out their fear by emptying their bowels. The custom continued and, as is the nature of such beliefs, grew in importance over the years until 1998 when Ronaldo didn't to go through with it. The sight of the bloated out of form young superstar waddling around the pitch was one of the talking points of the tournament and of particular concern to his team-mates several of whom were believers in macumba, the Brazilian twist on voodoo. That is only one of many conspiracy theories 'explaining' Ronaldo's behaviour at France 1998 but Brazilian football is rife with ritual from the 'religious icons' carried in the 'lucky brown suit' of Paulo Cavalho of the successful 1950s sides to the antics of Carlito Rocha in the league. The latter embraced sacred foods and ways of eating them; holy herb scented showers and tied up the curtains at half time to bewitch the legs of the opposition.

The reference to concentrações above links to a movement, Santo Daime, that started in Brazil in the 1920s and has supporters all over the world and, if one practitioner is to be believed, a profound effect on Mexican football. Santo Daime (literally meaning the holy give me) incorporates elements of Christianity, spiritism, shamanic belief and the imbibing of the herb ayahuasca. The powerful plant is used is both types of the sect's concentrações the vigourous bailados dances and more subdued hinarios or hymnals. It was a variation on this that Mexican shaman Angel Ochoa used to resurrect the fortunes of his side Necaxa in the 1990s.

Every league has a Necaxa (nicknamed the hidro-rayos -lightening bolts- after they were formed from a light and power company in 1923) who perform great feats then fade into the background slightly. For Necaxa it was the once hermanos (eleven brothers) era of the 1930s when they won successive championships from 1933 to 1938. Post war the side adapted badly to new professionalism of Mexican football and despite winning the odd cup and the championship in 1966 struggled to keep afloat financially and in the 1980s had several relegation scraps. By the nineties though fans were talking of the epoca Necaxista, a new golden age.

Some attributed this resurgence to the financial muscle and wise appointments provided by new owners, others the talents of coach Roberto Saporitti but Angel Ochoa believes his intervention turned the tables, or rather put Necaxa on top of the table. In the 1990s as well as three Mexican titles, they won the cup and international honours finishing higher than any Mexican ever has in the World Club Cup beating Real Madrid en route. Angel brought in a Wixáritari shaman whose rituals go back millennia to the time when the sacred ball game tlachtli was played. Happily Angel did not import all aspects of this mix of football, volleyball and religion as in tlachtli the losing side was occasionally sacrificed to the Sun God in whose honour the game was played.

Together with the shaman and an itinerant medicine man he spread peyote and ayahuasca through the Aztec Stadium which at the time was Necaxas' home. They opened the doors to the four guardians (as in wicca the points of the compass) and began their concentrações based on Santo Daime with sections of Necaxas' support which at this point was a mere five thousand in a stadium built for over hundred thousand. Angel is adamant that his actions brought the favour of the gods to Necaxa and certainly his actions in the early 1990s are followed by the new era of success and without recourse to sacrifice demanded in tlatchi.

In ancient Mexico a great deal was made of the links between the ball and the sun and tlatchi has been likened to an astrological study dressed up as a sport as the priests used the path of ball in the game to predict future movements in the heavens. It might therefore seem logical somehow for modern Mexicans to mix their football with other beliefs but what excuse do contemporary Australians have? Quite a lot if reports on the activities of comedian John Safran are anything to go by. Safran is credited by some as the real reason Australia qualified for 2006 World Cup by lifting a curse placed on them by a Mozambique witch doctor in 1969.

Former player Johnny Warren had told Safran that the struggling Aussie side won a playoff against Rhodesia after engaging a witchdoctor for £1000 but welshed on the deal. The witch doctor then cursed the team who lost to Israel in the final qualifier and suffered a series of improbable mishaps even when they did qualify. Warren clearly believed in the curse and cited it in his unlikely titled biography *Sheilas, Wogs and Poofters*, claiming that 'the bad luck always seems to come in big matches. Every time some disaster befalls our national teams I think back to Mozambique. I can't help wondering if there's something extraordinary to blame.'

Safran journeyed to Mozambique and engaged another witchdoctor (the original having died) to channel the spirit of the deceased priest to re-enact and reverse the curse. This involved sitting in the middle of the Telstra Stadium, where the game had been played, slaughtering a chicken and washing the blood off with clay.

In Argentina, being more modern and sophisticated, there was the odd case of the kidnapping of referee, Telemaco Xavier, in 1963. Allegedly he was taken by three men who came out of a silvery disc, a strange case of extra terrestrial forces taking a hand in football just as the gods of ancient Greece did in other sports. At least that is how they are portrayed in the film Jason and the Argonauts, like Olympian sized far Eastern betting syndicates intervening. This idea, that the gods, not only could but did interfere in the affairs of men is key to many belief systems and obviously football being one of mankind's most passionate affairs it would seem logical that they might get involved with that too. It should be said though that there have been no white bulls sacrificed to Zeus recently to influence the outcome of the Hellenic league.

The Grecians in the English League (Exeter City whose nickname relates to people from the parish of St. Sidwell who co-founded the club) called in paranormal help in the form of Uri Gellor. He, in a gesture very similar to some of the African examples above, placed crystals behind the goals at Exeter's ground before a vital match against Chester City. The Grecians lost five to one but magic knows no boundaries and they were saved from relegation by other results going their way. Not to be outdone Raquel Bailey who supports fellow West Country side Yeovil Town cast a 'cross-legged spell' on Charlton Athletic ahead of an FA Cup tie. Rather disingenuously Bailey denied any sinister intent just hoping that 'something funny' would happen to the team's legs when they approach the goalmouth. In all events it failed as Charlton beat Yeovil 3-2, with one commentator ironically stating that: 'Charlton have struggled against lesser teams in cup matches but they finally broke their jinx.'

Given Charlton's plummet down the league pyramid perhaps the spell was a slow burner and despite Gellor's antics Exeter were relegated from the football league in 2002 under his stewardship. Geller was not even in the ground, never mind laying totems around the pitch, for his own, self declared, most famous sporting moment. This was to use his psychic powers to shift the ball from under Gary McAllister's feet when taking a penalty against England causing him to miss.

No magic is usually required to make English penalty takers miss but in the 2006 World Cup one side thought they'd take no chances. The story goes that in the run up to England's match against an Ecuador team competing in their first finals the Latin Americans got a little extra help from a shaman, Tzamarenda Naychapi. This Ecuadorian witchdoctor visited Stuttgart's Gottlieb-Daimler-Stadium to rid it of evil spirits and bring positive energy to his team. He is also supposed to have cursed the opposing team so that they would under perform. Not to be outdone East London wiccan Brian Botham performed a counter curse on live TV, because let's face it we do know a thing or too about occult powers in this country as well. Brian constructed a relatively simple spell that was magnified by his quartz crystal wand laid over an England squad picture and the studio audience. After he chanted put fire in their hearts and thunder in their belly through the power of the telly send this spell to England. He asked the audience to echo his affirmation of the chant by saying so mote it be. Prior this he performed a cleansing spell to lift the curse, sprinkling sage and salt water he used the four elements to remove the Ecuadorian enchantment. This spell ran; fire to cleanse and purge his spell, water to wish our England team well, earth to hold it good and true and air to blow it back to you.

Brian's spell appeared to work; at least it was not in any way, as the sceptics say, contradicted by reality. One of the stranger results of this counter curse were the famous images of David Beckham vomiting out the evil of the first curse onto the pitch and then going on to hit a beautiful free kick to win the match. As the team's talisman it is natural that Brian's spell would have worked most powerfully through Beckham. In fact it might, of course, have been better still if Brian's spell had lifted the uselessness curse on a few of the other players too. There was a less successful attempt in the previous World Cup by some Druids at Stonehenge to influence the result of the Brazil versus

England game. The game kicked off shortly after dawn Greenwich Mean Time on the day after the solstice, one of the holiest days for the old British religion. A positive energy wave was summoned up for the English team and directed across the world. Unfortunately it either hit the wrong team or it was a case of druids 0 juju 2.

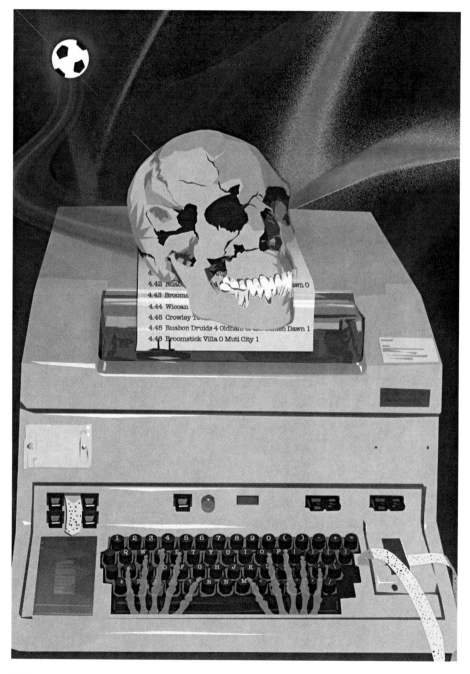

Final score

L ike the Saturday afternoon results service this brief chapter isn't really, what with the 5.15 kick off and Sunday games, the last word, and, like many football related experiences, may prove a bit of a let down. This is because, unlike the game itself, there is no definitive result with this magic stuff. All kinds of research points to the fact that correct mental preparation positively influences a player's performance and that strong faith can enhance a team's. There are also a number of studies into the effects of colour, home advantage and other factors which can raise a side up, but there is no spell which works for everyone in all circumstances just a selection of firm beliefs held by a disparate community who want to gain some sort of advantage.

In the run up to the 2010 World Cup there have been strenuous efforts by some involved in the game's administration to steer away from the paranormal (of all types) in direct contrast to modern players being more overtly religious than for some time. Both groups are responding to different pressures which exist within global football. Players are asked to perform ever greater feats on the pitch and the media scrutiny off it means that they are required to develop legal means to cope with both. Firm faith can be a very useful thing in this context however FIFA President Sepp Blatter fears that overt religious expression in football may make it appear sectarian and therefore diminish the global appeal. The example given on BBC radio's Heart and Soul programme was of a devout Christian player, Kaka say, scoring the winning goal in a World Cup played in Muslim country and celebrating by revealing a Christian t- shirt.

There is, as mentioned in the chapter on juju, a longer standing issue being faced by the various African Football Federations trying to rid the game of links with voodoo. It would appear that progress has been made as no fresh stories emerged from the 2010 African Cup of Nations but the issue in sub Saharan Africa is complicated by several national associations using witches in the past and players adopting their own extreme rituals. Focus on juju from the western media is a bit unfair because the developing field of sports psychology in Europe is starting to measure the efficacy of all sorts of pre match rituals from a 'scientific' point of view.

A decent case can be made that players do perform better if they are mentally prepared and that ritualised behavior can help this process. There is a lot less evidence that magic in the form of spells by outside parties work directly but plenty of examples worldwide where it has been tried and appeared to make a difference. The practices may vary from burying cats under a stadium in Buenos Aires to hiring a witch in Bucharest but the core belief in something other than fitness and ball skills being able to alter the outcome of a match are the same. There are of course a massive number of examples where rituals appear not to work but, just as atheists tend to be less strident as death approaches, so few players (or supporters) faced with relegation are unwilling to at least try something literally leftfield.

In a sense that is the final result because as long as people follow teams and invest their hopes, dreams and passions in football an aspect of that will be devoted to prayer, sacrifice and ritual. As long as people are superstitious and magically think that their actions can have an influence there will be thousands of people every Saturday donning lucky pants, leaving the house by the back door and eating unlikely pics for breakfast. Likewise as players continue to believe that every little thing can help there will be those entering the pitch late, peeing in odd places and burying the odd frog. In the end if the final score is positive then, for a short time, there is proof of magic working.

Select bibliography

Occasionally when I felt a story was so outrageous it required clear citation there are specific references to newspapers and journals in the text. Mostly however the information was culled from a widespread (if rather chaotic) searching of football sites on the Internet, personal interviews* and studying of some beautifully obscure sports psychology and folklore publications.

This book would not exist without the hard work put in by Gary designing it and Daniel and Andy providing the images. I would also like to thank Geraldine from Atlantis and Christina of Treadwells (the Celtic and Rangers of London occult bookshops) for their help as well as Joanne and the numerous other people who read the various early versions of *Football Voodoo* and added in their own comments and corrections.

I would also like to thank Geraldine from Atlantis and Christina of Treadwells (the Celtic and Rangers of London occult bookshops) for their help as well as Joanne and the numerous other people who read the various early versions of Football Voodoo and added in their own comments and corrections. I should say however that any tactical errors or poor selections which remain are my responsibility and mine alone.

This might be the place as well to apologise for any inherent bias in the anecdotes included which are the result of where I started watching the game and era I grew up in. I should also add to any strict followers of the left hand path that I have been rather free with my use of certain terms relating to the occult which a purist might quibble at but essentially in the text juju, muti, voodoo and the various South American terms for such practices are used interchangeably.

The books I found most useful however listed below in no particular order.

Iona Opie, 1992. *A Dictionary of Superstitions*. Oxford Reference.
James Frazer, 1996. *The Golden Bough: A Study in Magic and Religion*. Penguin.
Alex Bellos, 2003. *Futebol: The Brazilian Way of Life* Bloomsbury Publishing.

*it's not every project that legitimizes interviewing a Mexican shaman or indeed a voodoo priestess in a south London coffee shop.

When Saturday Comes, 2006. *When Saturday Comes: The Half Decent Football.* Penguin.

Filippo Maria Ricci, 2008. *Lions Elephants, Lions and Eagles: A Journey Through African Football.* When Saturday Comes.

Desmond Morris, 1981. *The Soccer Tribes.* Jonathan Cape Ltd.

Mark Roques, 2003. *Fields of God: Football and the Kingdom of God.* Authentic Lifestyle.

Alan Edge, 2009. *Faith of our fathers: Football as a Religion.* Mainstream.

Chris Taylor, 1998. *The Beautiful Game: Journey Through Latin American Football.* Weidenfeld & Nicolson.

Mark Reynolds (Editor), 1998. *The Wrong Kind of Shirts: Bk. 3* Fourth Estate Ltd.

Ian Hawkey , 2009, *Feet of the Chameleon: History of African Football.* Portico.

Michael Goss. October 1996. *Cursed Football: Why your team will never win the cup.* Fortean Times FT91. Fortean Times : London

Index

Lightning Source UK Ltd.
Milton Keynes UK
27 May 2010

154827UK00001B/81/P